Maintaining Institutional Integrity

Donald E. Puyear, George B. Vaughan, *Editors*

NEW DIRECTIONS FOR COMMUNITY COLLEGES
ARTHUR M. COHEN, *Editor-in-Chief*
FLORENCE B. BRAWER, *Associate Editor*

Number 52, December 1985

Paperback sourcebooks in
The Jossey-Bass Higher Education Series

Jossey-Bass Inc., Publishers
San Francisco • London

Donald E. Puyear, George B. Vaughan (Eds.).
Maintaining Institutional Integrity.
New Directions for Community Colleges, no. 52.
Volume XIII, number 4.
San Francisco: Jossey-Bass, 1985.

New Directions for Community Colleges
Arthur M. Cohen, *Editor-in-Chief;* Florence B. Brawer, *Associate Editor*

New Directions for Community Colleges (publication number USPS 121-710) is published quarterly by Jossey-Bass Inc., Publishers, San Francisco, CA 94104, in association with the ERIC Clearinghouse for Junior Colleges. *New Directions* is numbered sequentially—please order extra copies by sequential number. The volume and issue numbers above are included for the convenience of libraries. Second class postage rates paid at San Francisco, California, and at additional mailing offices.

The material in this publication was prepared pursuant to a contract with the National Institute of Education, U.S. Department of Education. Contractors undertaking such projects under government sponsorship are encouraged to express freely their judgment in professional and technical matters. Prior to publication, the manuscript was submitted to the Center for the Study of Community Colleges for critical review and determination of professional competence. This publication has met such standards. Points of view or opinions, however, do not necessarily represent the official view or opinions of the Center for the Study of Community Colleges or the National Institute of Education.

Correspondence:
Subscriptions, single-issue orders, change of address notices, undelivered copies, and other correspondence should be sent to Subscriptions, Jossey-Bass Inc., Publishers, 433 California Street, San Francisco, California 94104.

Editorial correspondence should be sent to the Editor-in-Chief, Arthur M. Cohen, at the ERIC Clearinghouse for Junior Colleges, University of California, Los Angeles, California 900024.

Library of Congress Catalog Card Number 85-60827

International Standard Serial Number ISSN 0194-3081

International Standard Book Number ISBN 87589-742-8

Cover art by WILLI BAUM

Manufactured in the United States of America

This publication was prepared with funding from the National Institute of Education, U.S. Department of Education, under contract no. 400-83-0030. The opinions expressed in the report do not necessarily reflect the positions or policies of NIE or the Department.

Ordering Information

The paperback sourcebooks listed below are published quarterly and can be ordered either by subscription or single-copy.

Subscriptions cost $40.00 per year for institutions, agencies, and libraries. Individuals can subscribe at the special rate of $30.00 per year *if payment is by personal check*. (Note that the full rate of $40.00 applies if payment is by institutional check, even if the subscription is designated for an individual.) Standing orders are accepted.

Single copies are available at $9.95 when payment accompanies order, and *all single-copy orders under $25.00 must include payment*. (California, New Jersey, New York, and Washington, D.C., residents please include appropriate sales tax.) For billed orders, cost per copy is $9.95 plus postage and handling. (Prices subject to change without notice.)

Bulk orders (ten or more copies) of any individual sourcebook are available at the following discounted prices: 10–49 copies, $8.95 each; 50–100 copies, $7.96 each; over 100 copies, *inquire*. Sales tax and postage and handling charges apply as for single copy orders.

To ensure correct and prompt delivery, all orders must give either the *name of an individual* or an *official purchase order number*. Please submit your order as follows:

Subscriptions: specify series and year subscription is to begin.
Single Copies: specify sourcebook code (such as, CC1) and first two words of title.

Mail orders for United States and Possessions, Latin America, Canada, Japan, Australia, and New Zealand to:
Jossey-Bass Inc., Publishers
433 California Street
San Francisco, California 94104

Mail orders for all other parts of the world to:
Jossey-Bass Limited
28 Banner Street
London EC1Y 8QE

New Directions for Community Colleges Series
Arthur M. Cohen, *Editor-in-Chief*
Florence B. Brawer, *Associate Editor*

CC1 *Toward a Professional Faculty,* Arthur M. Cohen
CC2 *Meeting the Financial Crisis,* John Lombardi
CC3 *Understanding Diverse Students,* Dorothy M. Knoell
CC4 *Updating Occupational Education,* Norman C. Harris

CC5   *Implementing Innovative Instruction,* Roger H. Garrison
CC6   *Coordinating State Systems,* Edmund J. Gleazer, Jr., Roger Yarrington
CC7   *From Class to Mass Learning,* William M. Birenbaum
CC8   *Humanizing Student Services,* Clyde E. Blocker
CC9   *Using Instructional Technology,* George H. Voegel
CC10 *Reforming College Governance,* Richard C. Richardson, Jr.
CC11 *Adjusting to Collective Bargaining,* Richard J. Ernst
CC12 *Merging the Humanities,* Leslie Koltai
CC13 *Changing Managerial Perspectives,* Barry Heermann
CC14 *Reaching Out Through Community Service,* Hope M. Holcomb
CC15 *Enhancing Trustee Effectiveness,* Victoria Dziuba, William Meardy
CC16 *Easing the Transition from Schooling to Work,* Harry F. Silberman, Mark B. Ginsburg
CC17 *Changing Instructional Strategies,* James O. Hammons
CC18 *Assessing Student Academic and Social Progress,* Leonard L. Baird
CC19 *Developing Staff Potential,* Terry O'Banion
CC20 *Improving Relations with the Public,* Louis W. Bender, Benjamin R. Wygal
CC21 *Implementing Community-Based Education,* Ervin L. Harlacher, James F. Gollatscheck
CC22 *Coping with Reduced Resources,* Richard L. Alfred
CC23 *Balancing State and Local Control,* Searle F. Charles
CC24 *Responding to New Missions,* Myron A. Marty
CC25 *Shaping the Curriculum,* Arthur M. Cohen
CC26 *Advancing International Education,* Maxwell C. King, Robert L. Breuder
CC27 *Serving New Populations,* Patricia Ann Walsh
CC28 *Managing in a New Era,* Robert E. Lahti
CC29 *Serving Lifelong Learners,* Barry Heermann, Cheryl Coppeck Enders, Elizabeth Wine
CC30 *Using Part-Time Faculty Effectively,* Michael H. Parsons
CC31 *Teaching the Sciences,* Florence B. Brawer
CC32 *Questioning the Community College Role,* George B. Vaughan
CC33 *Occupational Education Today,* Kathleen F. Arns
CC34 *Women in Community Colleges,* Judith S. Eaton
CC35 *Improving Decision Making,* Mantha Mehallis
CC36 *Marketing the Program,* William A. Keim, Marybelle C. Keim
CC37 *Organization Development: Change Straategies,* James Hammons
CC38 *Institutional Impacts on Campus, Community, and Business Constituencies,* Richard L. Alfred
CC39 *Improving Articulation and Transfer Relationships,* Frederick C. Kintzer
CC40 *General Education in Two-Year Colleges,* B. Lamar Johnson
CC41 *Evaluating Faculty and Staff,* Al Smith
CC42 *Advancing the Liberal Arts,* Stanley F. Turesky
CC43 *Counseling: A Crucial Function for the 1980s,* Alice S. Thurston, William A. Robbins
CC44 *Strategic Management in the Community College,* Gunder A. Myran
CC45 *Designing Programs for Community Groups,* S. V. Martorana, William E. Piland
CC46 *Emerging Roles for Community College Leaders,* Richard L. Alfred, Paul A. Elsner, R. Jan LeCroy, Nancy Armes
CC47 *Microcomputer Applications in Administration and Instruction,* Donald A. Dellow, Lawrence H. Poole

CC48 *Customized Job Training for Business and Industry,* Robert J. Kopecek, Robert G. Clarke
CC49 *Ensuring Effective Governance,* William L. Deegan, James F. Gollattscheck
CC50 *Strengthening Financial Management,* Dale F. Campbell
CC51 *Active Trusteeship for a Changing Era,* Gary Frank Petty

Contents

Editors' Notes   1
Donald E. Puyear, George B. Vaughan

Chapter 1. The Search for Mission and Integrity:
A Retrospective View   3
Jennings L. Wagoner, Jr.
The community college, "untrammeled by tradition," must face its past as it confronts its present condition and pursues its search for mission and integrity in the future.

Chapter 2. Maintaining Open Access and Comprehensiveness   17
George B. Vaughan
If the community college is to maintain its integrity, it must be true to its philosophy and mission, which should be built on open access, and it must articulate its mission and philosophy to its constituents in an effective and consistent manner.

Chapter 3. General Threats to Institutional Integrity   29
Gordon K. Davies
Threats to institutional integrity can come from within or without. Major threats are the avoidance of difficult management decisions and the failure to control and direct change.

Chapter 4. Parttime Faculty: Integrity and Integration   37
Judith L. McGaughey
Whether a faculty member is full- or parttime may be irrelevant to the question of the impact of all faculty members on institutional or academic integrity.

Chapter 5. Maintaining Faculty Vitality   49
Thelma C. Altshuler, Suzanne L. Richter
Maintaining faculty vitality in the face of heavy teaching loads and the unrelenting challenge of underprepared students requires conscious effort and planning on the part of faculty members and academic administrators.

Chapter 6. Maintaining Integrity in a State System   63
Donald E. Puyear
Increasing state control, which is adding to the complexity of community college governance, requires new skills of community college leaders.

Chapter 7. Sources and Information:
Maintaining Institutional Integrity 77
Jim Palmer, Diane Zwemer

Index 103

Editors' Notes

For the past two decades, the direction taken by community colleges has been influenced by any number of movements — some of which consisted of little more than using catch words or phrases to capture the concern of the day. Each year has a different catch phrase — the open door, the "movement," the student as consumer, measurable objectives, community-based, competency-based, accountability — the list goes on. The point is that the community college, like much of the rest of higher education, interacts with forces that extend beyond the campus.

Today, the rallying call for community colleges is quality. Politicians, educators, the media, and the public are demanding that educational institutions offer quality education.

While it is important that community college leaders be sensitive to current trends in higher education and in society, there is some danger in following trends too slavishly. For example, as suggested above, the quality issue is currently in vogue and is indeed an important issue for community colleges. Yet the umbrella under which the issue of quality must fall, as with most other issues, is that of maintaining institutional integrity in accordance with the college's mission. The key issue facing community college leaders today and in the future is and will be how to maintain institutional integrity and at the same time adapt the college's mission to a changing environment.

In this volume, the issue of maintaining institutional integrity is addressed from a variety of perspectives in the hope that this will provide community college leaders and others who make state policy with information that will be useful as they face the challenge of adapting community colleges to today's and tomorrow's environment.

Donald E. Puyear
George B. Vaughan
Editors

Donald E. Puyear is deputy chancellor of the Virginia Community College System. Prior to assuming his current position, in 1983 he was president of Central Virginia Community College.

George B. Vaughan is president of Piedmont Virginia Community College and author of numerous articles and books on the community college.

The community college, "untrammeled by tradition," must face its past as it confronts its present condition and pursues its search for mission and integrity in the future.

The Search for Mission and Integrity: A Retrospective View

Jennings L. Wagoner, Jr.

Since the birth of the junior college/community college movement, various spokesmen have articulated an ever expanding list of functions and missions for these two-year institutions. Because of significant shifts in focus and direction that have occurred over time, throughout much of its history the junior/community college has been uncertain of its identity, unsure of its place in the postsecondary community, and unable to determine its institutional priorities. Reform of the institution has been incremental in nature, characterized by the addition of new services and adoption of new functions in response to real or perceived public demands or needs. Recently heralded as "the most important educational institution of the mid-twentieth century" (McCabe, 1981, p. 7), the community college, in the closing decades of this century, is facing challenges and constraints that already suggest that the golden age of the community college movement is now clearly in the past (Vaughan, 1983).

In Search of Foundations

Historically, the junior/community college has faced the future more than the past or the present. Its supporting ideology and its eagerness to accept more and more functions have typically rested on a promise of future accomplishments. Even so, the past has held a special attraction for some supporters of the junior/community college concept. Often less concerned with historical understanding or analysis than with the identification of antecedents that hold promise of conferring the legitimacy of age on the two-year college, community college publicists have been untiring in their search for the first or oldest forerunner of the modern institution. While there is general agreement that the first public junior college was organized at Joliet, Illinois, in 1901, there is less certainty about the origin of the private junior college. Among the most commonly mentioned contenders for the title for the first private junior college are the Lewis Institute of Chicago, founded in 1896, Lasell Female Seminary (later Lasell Junior College) established in Massachusetts in 1851, and, in what is indeed a far stretch, the foundation of the first Catholic college in Newton, Maryland in 1677—a century before the nation itself was born (Palinchak, 1973).

Debate surrounding the institutional foundations of the two-year college is matched in imagination if not in intensity by attempts to discover the intellectual foundations of the movement. Perhaps the most ambitious leap of imagination in this regard was that noted by a former executive director of the American Association of Junior Colleges, Walter Crosby Eells, who commented, "There are those who would trace the beginnings of the junior college movement... to the Renaissance... in the sixteenth century" (Palinchak, 1973, p. 21).

Few chroniclers of the junior/community college movement have felt inclined to fashion a history from Renaissance origins. However, many have identified currents and leaders in the American educational past that might be said to have provided spiritual if not substantive nourishment for what must in reality be considered a twentieth-century development. If one accepts as a beginning premise Brick's (1964) assertion that four basic social and economic forces led to the junior college idea—equality of opportunity, use of education to achieve social mobility, technological progress, and acceptance of the concept that education is the producer of social capital—then one is surely not hard pressed to identify numerous articulate spokesmen and developments. From Benjamin Franklin's advice regarding adult self-education and his founding of the Philadelphia Academy, to Thomas Jefferson's stress on the importance of careers open to all with talent and his efforts to establish a comprehensive system of education in Virginia, and on to Justin Morrill's advocacy of land-grant colleges that offered practical as well as theoretical instruction, the intellectual if not the institutional foundations of an increasingly democratic and expanding system of education were well laid out long before the junior/community college was born.

There is much to be gained from the study of the ideas and actions of these and other educational pioneers who in various ways may be said to have possessed a philosophical kinship with later champions of the junior/community college movement. However, there is also the danger that exaggerating linkages and of appropriating ideals and rhetoric concerning the junior/community college can obscure its real beginnings and deflect attention from a critical appraisal of its pervading ideology, changing missions, and continuing search for identity and integrity.

Early Form and Function of the Junior College

Although the junior/community college is a twentieth century institution, several educational leaders began drafting sketches of a postsecondary, preuniversity type of college in the nineteenth century. Henry P. Tappan of the University of Michigan in the 1850s and William Watts Folwell of the University of Minnesota in the 1870s both advocated a reorganization of higher education that would lead to the separation of the freshman and sophomore years from the higher levels of university study. Dissatisfied with the inferior quality of American colleges when compared to the nineteenth century German universities, these state university presidents were far less concerned with developing a rationale for junior colleges than with creating true universities dedicated to the highest levels of scholarship. In essence, Tappan and Folwell wanted to amputate the first two collegiate years from the university body, a surgical procedure also advocated by other university spokesmen well into the twentieth century.

Concern for the health and vitality of the emerging American university must be recognized as an important factor influencing the birth and development of the junior/community college idea in the United States. However, those who around the turn of the century took up the task of transforming earlier sketches into more complete architectural plans for an equally vigorous junior college added new rationales in support of the two-year college. Specifically, William Rainey Harper, David Starr Jordan, and Alexis F. Lange envisioned the junior college as not only accepting the function of providing the general education being deemphasized by research-oriented universities, but saw in the new junior college the potential for providing stability in a society impressed with the need for order and efficiency. These architects of the junior college sought to bestow a degree of legitimacy on and give integrity to the junior college. They did so by enveloping the new institution in an ideology peculiarly suited to the demands of an increasingly impersonal and industrializing nation that was in search of organizing principles around which a viable social order could be constructed (Wiebe, 1967).

Architects of the Junior College

William Rainey Harper, who became the first president of the Rockefeller-endowed University of Chicago in 1891, is credited with being the father of the junior college. The reorganized university opened in 1892 with two divisions, a university college encompassing the junior and senior years and an academic college for the freshman and sophomore levels. In 1896, Harper substituted the terms *senior college* and *junior college* for the earlier terms. Although the distinction between junior and senior work that existed in Harper's mind was not consistently followed in practice at Chicago, he persuaded the faculty and trustees in 1900 to institute an Associate Degree to be awarded students who completed the prescribed work of the junior college. Harper's efforts in creating a distinctive junior college division within the University of Chicago and his more indirect but no less important influence surrounding the development of Joliet Junior College and a similar but short-lived institution in Goshen, Indiana, certainly merit for him the title of father of the junior college. However, like Tappan and Folwell earlier, Harper was more concerned with the purity of the university than with the form of the junior college. Harper did not lay out a design for the junior college as a single type of institution. He advocated at various times the upward extension of high school work into the thirteenth and fourteenth years, the transformation of small, struggling four-year colleges and teachers' institutes into two-year institutions, or, as in the case of Chicago, the separate organization within a university of the first two years of collegiate study.

To Harper, function was more important than form. In institutional terms, the immediate function of the junior college was to offer instruction of the same nature as that typically offered to freshmen and sophomores in the leading colleges and universities. The junior college would thus mark the natural division between a general and specialized program of study for those who would continue their education into the university realm. For those who by interest or ability were not suited for university study, the junior college would offer an acceptable terminal point for their general educational pursuits. Invoking a democratic theme that has long been a constant in the junior/community college ideology, Harper also stressed the view that the junior college with its associate degree would encourage many more students to undertake two additional years of collegiate study (Harper, 1900).

Even more important for Harper than institutional arrangements and individual benefits were the social functions of the fledgling junior college. The order and efficiency Harper was trying to introduce into the academic world reflected his desire, shared by many progressive reformers of his day, to put in place the machinery that would ensure structure, order, and efficiency in the larger society. As a historian of the University of Chicago observed, Harper's "revulsion against disorder in education" and his "admiration for devices calculated to make education more efficient" reflected his concern for the more harmonious functioning of the larger society (Storr, 1966, p. 214). To Harper, then, the mission of the junior college and a yardstick by which to measure its integrity rested in its ability to contribute to the stability of the social order by enabling the individual to discover "the thing nature intended for him to do" (Harper, 1895, p. 987) and by equipping him to occupy successfully and productively his proper niche in society. Anticipating the role that guidance and individualized instruction would later play in the junior/community college ideology, Harper emphasized the importance of "careful diagnosis" and proper placement of students (Harper, 1905, pp. 317–326).

David Starr Jordan and Alexis F. Lange, who with Harper must be considered as the prime architects of the junior college movement, shared many ideas in common with their Chicago colleague. Trained as a biologist and much impressed with the theory of evolution, Jordan held that the destiny of the human race rested with the "fittest" and feared that the masses, if not properly informed, could hold back the talented. Declaring that "you cannot fashion a two-thousand dollar education to a fifty-cent boy" (Jordan, 1896, p. 1), the president of Stanford feared that allowing the multitude into the university would "cheapen" and "vulgarize" higher education (p. 117). At the same time, Jordan often spoke of "the democracy of the intellect," by which he meant that all should have a fair chance to be educated to the limits of their abilities. To Jordan, the failure to lift an intelligent man from the masses was a case of human waste and inefficiency that amounted to a sin against society. Convinced that "every man that lives has a right to some form of higher education" (p. 68), Jordan, like Harper, nonetheless wanted to preserve the elite university as the crowning feature of the educational edifice. Although not as clear as Harper appeared to be regarding the proper timing of the end of general education and the beginning of specialized study, and less impressed with the German university model than some of his contemporaries, Jordan eventually came to view the junior college as the proper institution to provide socially useful education for the masses while at the same time protecting the university by weeding out "mock students" (Jordan, 1903, p. 146).

More clearly than either Harper or Jordan, Alexis F. Lange viewed the junior college as important not only in terms of the functions it might inherit from the university, but also as an evolving institutional form with a distinctive mission. As a faculty member of the University of California at Berkeley, Lange was involved in a committee recommendation that led to a division in lower and upper level studies in 1902. At one with Harper and Jordan in his estimation of the university's honored position atop the educational pyramid, Lange contributed significantly to the emerging junior/community college ideology by emphasizing the new institution's potential as the capstone of secondary education. In terms of form, the junior college as envisioned by Lange would be in effect an extended high school, separately organized and existing as "the dome of the secondary school edifice" rather than as "merely a university entrance hall or vestibule" (Lange, 1918, p. 211). Lange's concept of the junior college as a distinctly American institution deemphasized its role as a feeder to the university. In addition to this function, and even more important to Lange, was the junior college's mission of promoting social and vocational efficiency for those students not destined for university study and professional careers. Moreover, Lange moved beyond Harper and Jordan in emphasizing the integral relationship that should exist between the junior college and its surrounding community. Reflecting his alignment with progressive John Dewey, Lange maintained that the junior college as it matured should be part of the community, not isolated from it, and should strive to be "as widely and directly useful to the community as possible." Among community projects considered by Lange as appropriate undertakings for the junior college were conducting surveys, developing social centers, offering extension classes, arranging internships for students in public agencies, and offering adult education classes for immigrants preparing for citizenship (Lange, 1915, p. 447). The junior college concept advocated by Lange was already well on its way toward embracing the community services functions that in time became a staple of the two-year college mission.

Harper, Jordan, and Lange, differing though they did in particulars regarding the form and functions of the junior college, nonetheless approached their architectural work with a shared ideological commitment. Whether viewing the new institution as the foundation of higher education or the apex of secondary education, whether emphasizing its university preparatory function or its individual and social contributions, the basic goal each held before the junior college was responsiveness to the ideal of a more efficient, orderly, and rationalized educational system and social order.

Setting the Foundations for the Junior College

By the end of World War I, the junior college idea, variously interpreted, had spread to many parts of the nation. Confusion as to the form and function of the junior college was underscored in a 1919 report issued by the Bureau of Education in which it was noted that the junior college was still in an experimental stage. The author of the report lamented that "We do not know what it should be, because we do not know what it is. Before we can see clearly what it is, we must know why it is" (McDowell, 1919, pp. 6–7).

Concern over the what and why of the junior college was addressed, but by no means resolved, at a meeting of junior college leaders in 1920. At the time of this initial meeting of what emerged the following year as the American Association of Junior Colleges (AAJC), there were approximately 175 institutions, mostly private, laying claim to uncertain status as junior colleges (Brick, 1964, p. 29). Discussions at the 1920 conference revealed sharp divisions among those seeking to achieve definition, recognition, and status for the junior college. Some, like conference chairman James M. Wood, argued for a four-year junior college, an institution that would combine the upper secondary school grades with the lower two years of collegiate education. Others took exception to Wood's plan that would also allow the four-year junior college to confer a baccalaureate degree and maintained that the junior college should be defined as a two-year institution authorized to award associate degrees only. More familiar points of debate centered on the question of whether the junior college represented a continuation of secondary schooling or the beginning of collegiate education. The U.S. Commissioner of Education, P. P. Claxton, informed the conferees that, in his view, the junior college role was still that of a selective agency for the "higher institutions," a buffer that should prevent state universities from being swamped with underclassmen. When in 1921 the AAJC adopted a formal constitution, agreement had been reached only to the extent that the junior college was then defined as "an institution offering two years of instruction of strictly collegiate grade" (Brick, 1964, pp. 33–34).

Subsequent annual meetings of the AAJC and its successor, the

American Association of Community and Junior Colleges (AACJC), continued to be sparked by debates over identity and status, form and function. In the period between the end of World War I and the outbreak of World War II, the focus of debates over mission and integrity began to widen, both as a consequence of the increase in the number of junior colleges and an expanding definition of functions deemed proper for the two-year institution. However, the underlying assumptions that formed the basis for the junior/community college ideology — an institution that would respond to the national quest for an orderly, efficient, and stratified educational and social system — remained constant (Goodwin, 1972).

Probably no single topic received more attention from junior college spokesmen during the interwar years than the maturing institution's need to provide "terminal education" for the large majority of students who were not bound for university study. A new generation of junior college enthusiasts popularized the idea that terminal education, defined as encompassing both vocational training and general education, should become the centerpiece of the junior college's mission. An early and persistent advocate of the primacy of the terminal mission was Leonard V. Koos, who in 1924 published the results of a detailed study of the nation's junior colleges. Koos reported that the junior college was already moving beyond its original conception of being an institution primarily concerned with the transfer function. To Koos, the key to understanding and advancing the junior college movement lay in appreciating its role in democratizing higher education. "Mental democratization" was the term Koos used to suggest that all youth had a right to receive education "suitable to their intellect" and he maintained that the junior college was the proper institution for that class of students who were to enter the "semi-professions" (Koos, 1925, pp. 118-121). These students, Koos asserted, tended to begin their studies somewhat earlier than university students and in the junior college could remain under the influence of the home for a longer period of time, would be less likely to get lost in the more impersonal university environment, and could have more opportunities for involvement in activities that develop leadership traits and proper civic values.

Walter Crosby Eells, who in 1930 became the first editor of the *Junior College Journal*, was another of the new generation of spokesmen who emphasized the importance of the terminal function as the foundation of the junior college mission. Alarmed by research that indicated that over 90 percent of all California junior college students intended to transfer to senior institutions, Eells argued that only a much smaller percentage had a reasonable chance of success (Eells, 1929). In a highly influential textbook published in 1931, *The Junior College*, Eells stressed four functions the junior college ought to perform, functions that became the standard litany within the movement for decades thereafter. Similarly to Koos, Eells noted first of all the democratizing or "popularizing function" of the junior college, its service to the individual and society via its provision of extended educational opportunity for those intelligent enough to achieve semiprofessional status. The preparatory or transfer function was also acknowledged by Eells, although he cautioned that students' aspirations often outdistanced their ability and that perhaps many students who intended to transfer would benefit more from study in a terminal program. This concern caused Eells to place heaviest stress on the other two junior college functions — terminal programs and guidance activities. Proper guidance, he maintained, would channel more students into terminal programs that would in turn make them more successful in college, work, and life. He asserted that the university should prepare a few for leadership; the junior college had the heavy responsibility of preparing the many for "followship" (p. 29).

Koos and Eells were but two of a large number of influential educators whose views in the pre-World War II era broadened the base and the mission of the junior college by elevating in importance its terminal and guidance functions. Other functions were also advocated during this period — adult education and community service, for example — and rising enrollments during the Depression years underscored the role the institution was destined to play in times of job scarcity. By 1940 private junior colleges still outnumbered public junior colleges (317 private versus 258 public) although the public colleges enrolled over two-thirds of all junior college students (Eells, 1940).

In spite of rising enrollments in the public sector, an expanding agenda, and heavy emphasis by junior college leaders on the centrality of guidance and terminal programs, students continued to enroll, in the ratio of two to one, in university transfer programs even though only half or less typically continued with their education beyond the junior college (Goodwin, 1972). As the United States entered World War II, the junior college was still largely wedded in reality, although not in rhetoric, to the preparatory function advocated by the institution's original architects.

Building the Modern Community College

In the aftermath of World War II, American society seemed determined to abandon the constraints endured during twelve years of depression and four years of war. The baby boom of the postwar years was but one highly visible and significant manifestation of the increasing appetite of a consumer-oriented society. The fusion of demographic trends, government policy, and business interests into what one historian (Hodgson, 1976, p. 51) termed a "suburban-industrial complex" led to an almost insatiable demand for new homes, appliances, automobiles, and other goods and services.

As belief in the abundant society grew, so too did demands for educational access. Supported by the GI Bill, returning veterans pressed colleges for entrance, viewing access as a right or entitlement rather than a privilege. Junior colleges, which had welcomed adult students during the war years, found by 1947 that veterans accounted for about 40 percent of their enrollment (Goodwin, 1972). Almost at once, or so it seemed, the two-year institution was being embraced as a fully legitimate member of the American educational system.

Interest in the two-year college was fueled not only by demand, but also by media publicity, support from various national foundations, and, most significantly, by recommendations from educational commissions. In 1947, President Truman's Commission on Higher Education popularized the community college concept by recommending that states create a network of locally controlled colleges that would place higher education within commuting distance of the majority of Americans. The Truman Commission estimated that at least 49 percent of the population had the mental ability to complete fourteen years of study in general or vocational programs that would lead to either gainful employment or to advanced study (President's Commission, 1947; Vaughan, 1983).

The community college title, which had been advocated by some junior college leaders during the war years, reflected the ever broadening array of functions the two-year institution was adopting. At the forefront of the push for establishing the community college as a comprehensive, multi-purpose institution was Leland L. Medsker. Medsker, who before the war had encouraged closer links between the junior college and industry, called in the postwar decades for a greater commitment by the two-year institution to adult education and community service in addition to the functions already established. Concerned as were many of his predecessors and contemporaries about the high number of transfer students who failed to transfer, Medsker advocated redoubled emphasis on the guidance or student personnel function of the junior college. Medsker struck a responsive chord among those who saw the two-year institution as democracy's college or the people's college when he endorsed the addition of yet another function to the institution's list, the remedial or "salvage" function. Adoption of the salvage function, which had been noted as early as 1931 by Eells, enabled the institution to offer a second chance to those students whose prior educational experiences were less than encouraging (Medsker, 1960, p. 22).

By the 1960s, the community college had indeed entered its golden era. Although some technical institutes and private junior colleges resisted the seductive appeal to open the door and take up the comprehensive banner waved by the community college enthusiasts, the community college label and concept had essentially captured the two-year college movement. All across the nation, state legislators voted funding for the building of statewide community college systems. The AAJC received generous grants in the 1950s and 1960s from foundations such as the Carnegie Corporation and the Kellogg Foundation. These funds were used to underwrite special studies and to provide support for leadership programs and other projects. Students at all levels of higher education benefitted from the National Defense Education Act of 1958 and the Higher Education Acts and amendments of the 1960s and 1970s. The community college's apparent responsiveness to the needs or interests of individuals, their communities, and the larger society, combined with its low cost to those who sought its services, had placed the institution in a seemingly golden position.

A Season of Reassessment

The almost frantic growth of the community college began to subside in the mid-1970s at the same time that the larger society began to come to terms with the prospect that the society of abundance was being replaced by a society of scarcity. Many of the 1,219 two-year institutions that today tend to follow the lead of the AACJC (AACJC, 1985, p. 30) are faced with the spectre of declining enrollments, financial cutbacks, challenges to the open-door philosophy and comprehensive mission, mounting criticisms from those external to the enterprise, and growing expressions of a loss of direction from within. Perhaps it might have been expected that an institution so readily influenced by the currents of the social order must experience the ebb as well as the surge of changing tides. However, the community college, never really secure in its identity in the best of times, has ample reason to reassess its mission and raise questions concerning its integrity in these less settled times.

K. Patricia Cross recently speculated that a plateau in the community college movement may have been reached in the late 1970s and early 1980s. Anticipating a revival of energy and renewed sense of mission, she observed that "the old ideals that sparked enthusiasm and the sense of common purpose in community colleges have receded, and new ideals have not yet emerged to take their place" (Cross, 1981, p. 113). Whether a new mission for the community college is needed or will emerge remains to be seen. The more pressing matter facing community college leaders in the closing years of the 1980s is that of accommodating past promises to current realities. Through all of its twists and turns since the early days of this century, the two-year college has billed itself as a responsive institution, unencumbered by tradition. Its very breadth of mission and comprehensiveness of functions have worked against the establishment of priorities. Perhaps the time has now come in the community college movement when its leaders can best serve the institution and the society by assessing its future in light of its past, reconciling its mission with an ordering of priorities, and establishing its identity as ways are sought to maintain the institution's integrity. To fail to meet this challenge is to continue the risk of allowing external forces and pressures driven by concerns for efficiency, order, and rigid stratification to define the future mission of the community college. It would be an ironic new twist in the history of the community college if it should now become what it set out not to be: inflexible and unresponsive.

References

AACJC 1984 Annual Report. *Community and Junior College Journal.* 1985, *55*(7), 29–36.
Brick, M. *Forum and Focus for the Junior College Movement.* New York: Teachers College, Columbia University, 1964.
Cross, K. P., "Community Colleges on the Plateau." *Journal of Higher Education*, 1981, *52*(2), 113–123.
Eells, W. C. "California Junior Colleges Through the Eyes of Their Students." *Proceedings of the Tenth Annual AAJC Meeting.* Atlantic City, N.J., 1929.
Eells, W. C. (Ed.). *American Junior Colleges.* Washington, D.C.: American Council on Education, 1940.
Goodwin, G. L. "The Historical Development of the Community/Junior College Ideology: An Analysis and Interpretation of the Writings of Selected Community/Junior College National Leaders from 1890 to 1970." Unpublished doctoral dissertation, University of Illinois, 1972.
Harper, W. R. "Ideals of Educational Work." *NEA Journal of Proceedings*, 1895, *34*, 987–998.
Harper, W. R. "The Associate Degree." *Educational Review*, April, 1900, *19*(3), 412–415.
Harper, W. R. *The Trend in Higher Education.* Chicago: The University of Chicago Press, 1905.
Hodgson, G. *America in Our Time.* New York: Random House, 1976.
Jordan, D. S. *The Care and Culture of Men.* San Francisco: Whitaker & Ray, 1896.
Jordan, D. S. "University Tendencies in America." *Popular Science Monthly*, 1903, *43*, 141–148.
Koos, L. V. *The Junior College Movement.* Boston: Ginn, 1925.

Lange, A. F. "A Junior College Department of Civic Education." *School and Society*, 1915 *2*(39), 442–448.
Lange, A. F. "The Junior College—What Manner of Child Shall This Be?" *School and Society*, 1918, *7*(165) 211–216.
McCabe, R. H. "Now Is the Time to Reform the American Community College." *Community and Junior College Journal, 51*(8), 6–10.
McDowell, F. M. *The Junior College.* U.S. Bureau of Education Bulletin No. 35. Washington, D.C.: U.S. Government Printing Office, 1919.
Medsker, L. L. *The Junior College: Progress and Prospect.* New York: McGraw-Hill, 1960.
Palinchak, R. *The Evolution of the Community College.* Metuchen, N.J.: Scarecrow Press, 1973.
President's Commission on Higher Education. *Higher Education for American Democracy.* (6 vols.) Washington, D.C.: U.S. Government Printing Office, 1947.
Storr, R. J. *Harper's University: The Beginnings.* Chicago: The University of Chicago Press, 1966.
Vaughan, G. B. "Historical Perspective: President Truman Endorsed Community College Manifesto." *Community and Junior College Journal, 53*(7), 20–24.
Vaughan, G. B. and Associates. *Issues for Community College Leaders in a New Era.* San Francisco: Jossey-Bass, 1983.
Wiebe, R. H. *The Search for Order: 1877–1920.* New York: Hill and Wang, 1967.

Jennings L. Wagoner is director of the Center for the Study of Higher Education, University of Virginia.

If the community college is to maintain its integrity, it must be true to its philosophy and mission, which should be built on open access, and it must articulate its mission and philosophy to its constituents in an effective and consistent manner.

Maintaining Open Access and Comprehensiveness

George B. Vaughan

The American dream comes in many packages: the right to vote is symbolic of the nation's commitment to political freedom; the right to invest one's self and one's wealth as one pleases in a capitalistic, free enterprise system is the economic version; the right to move from the lowest to the highest level of society is the social fulfillment of the American dream. All dreams are elusive; the American dream is no exception. How much of the dream one achieves often depends on how well prepared one is for the pursuit. The way most Americans become prepared to pursue the American dream is through public education, particularly higher education. Without open access to educational opportunities at all levels, the American dream cannot become a reality for many of the nation's population. However, access to education means more than being able to enter an institution; access means that the institution's integrity is such that those who enter have a reasonable chance of succeeding.

Open access to educational opportunity was slow in coming to a nation that claimed from its birth that all men are created equal. Perhaps part of the problem was in how the nation defined equality: women, minorities, and certain other segments of society were not considered equal until relatively recently. Perhaps another part of the problem was in reconciling the nation's dreams of equality and achievement. The conflict between maintaining a highly selective system of higher education based on intellectual merit and one that accepted virtually all comers was especially troublesome to the nation. Confusing the issue of equality further was the nation's heritage of frontier machismo that claimed that in order to get ahead in American society all one had to do was work harder, longer, and better than the next person. In any event, the movement toward open access to higher education was, like most other broad-based movements in America, evolutionary rather than revolutionary.

The Evolving Democratization of Higher Education

Interestingly, a major step was taken toward broadening the base of higher education even before many states developed a system of public education at the elementary and high school levels. In 1862, Congress passed the Morrill Act that resulted in the establishment of the nation's land grant institutions. From that point forward, the nation's system of higher education would never be the same. Rejecting the belief that only the rich and well born should receive higher education, land grant colleges taught both students and subjects previously excluded from higher education. The philosophical base on which the land grant institutions rested had two major components: one was the belief that any white male who had the intelligence and academic preparation to obtain a college education should be provided the opportunity to do so; the second was the belief that higher education should teach practical subjects, including agriculture and mechanical arts. The land grant institutions were to be funded largely at public expense, with the impetus for their establishment coming from the federal government.

Although revolutionary for its day, viewed from today's perspective the Morrill Act was the first major step in the evolutionary process that resulted in today's commitment to open access to higher education. Moreover, the insistence that the curriculum be expanded to include public service offerings as well as courses and programs in engineering, agriculture, and any number of nontraditional (as defined by a departure from the liberal arts curriculums of the day) offerings established the concept that more people could profit from higher education than previously thought to be the case and that higher education offerings should be more comprehensive than in the past.

Moving from the Morrill Act of 1862 to the Servicemen's Readjustment Act of 1944, or the GI Bill of Rights as it is commonly known, there was a new dimension added to the nation's commitment to broadening the base of college attendance. The GI Bill not only encouraged individuals from all walks of life to attend college but paid their way to do so. The World War II GI Bill and similar acts to aid the veterans of the Korean and Vietnam wars left little doubt that the federal government was interested in higher education, not only as a way for individual improvement but also as a means of achieving a more open society. The nation's commitment to open access to higher education was taking shape.

A strong endorsement of open access to higher education came shortly after the end of the World War II. In 1947, the Report of the President's Commission on Higher Education for American Democracy was issued. Popularly known as the Truman Commission Report, it called for the availability of two years of education beyond high school for virtually all citizens. Indeed, the Commission members proclaimed that as many as 49 percent of the college-age youth could successfully complete at least two years of education beyond high school. A key to opening higher educational opportunities to virtually all Americans was to be a nationwide network of publicly supported two-year colleges, if the Commission's recommendations were followed. These community colleges, as the Commission called them, were to offer programs designed to qualify students to go to work at the end of two years or to transfer to a four-year institution to complete the bachelor's degree. The courses and programs offered by community colleges were to serve the needs of the community in which the colleges were located; the curriculums were to be comprehensive in the sense that students had a choice of entering an occupational curriculum (a terminal curriculum, as it was known prior to the advent of lifelong learning) or a transfer curriculum. Many of the students who enrolled at the local community college were the first members of their families ever to attend college. The door to educational opportunity was opening wider and wider.

Other events in post-World War II society contributed to the broadening of the base of higher education: the unparalleled affluence of American society made it possible for the nation to fund post-high school education for virtually everyone; an increasingly technical society made the community college, with its emphasis on technical programs, more appealing as an alternative to more traditional college programs; *Brown versus Board of Education* reminded the nation that equality of opportunity remained an elusive dream for a large segment of the American population almost ten years after America's second war that was to make the world safe for democracy had ended; and the launching of Sputnik in

1957 reminded the nation that democracies have no guaranteed foothold on scientific discovery.

While one can trace the thread of open access down any number of avenues, the confluence of three events finally made the American dream of open access to higher education a reality. First, the postwar baby boomers reached college age in the 1960s; unlike their parents, they never asked if higher education was a right or a privilege. The age-old question of who goes to college became passé; the new question of the 1960s was who goes where to college. Second, the open society of the political left became a reality during the 1960s as the nation moved to eliminate poverty and ignorance. Third, the Higher Education Act of 1965 and its later amendments, especially the 1972 amendments, made it possible for virtually everyone who could establish a need for financial assistance to receive such assistance.

The Community College and Open Access

No institution of higher education in the nation has made the commitment to open access to higher education more than the community college. Those state universities that are required by law to accept all high school graduates often reject almost as soon as they are enrolled those students who are academically ill-prepared; the City University of New York's experiment with open access to the university division during the 1970s has been largely aborted; the many essentially open door state colleges and private colleges cling to the myth of selectivity; only the public comprehensive community college has consistently and unequivocally committed itself to open access both in word and deed. Most community college mission statements call for the acceptance of all high school graduates and anyone who is eighteen years of age or older who can profit from attending the community college. Open access is the philosophical base on which the community college mission rests.

Comprehensiveness

Philosophical concepts, no matter how noble, have little meaning to most people unless they are translated into concrete terms. Translation of the community college's philosophy takes place largely through the college's comprehensive program and course offerings. Indeed, an open access institution that offers few or no choices to the student is a contradiction in terms.

In addition to its philosophy of open access and its commitment to a comprehensive academic program, the community college is committed to other concepts that help maintain and promote open access. Some of these concepts are: a commitment to guidance and counseling, a commitment to keeping costs low for the individual, a commitment to offering educational opportunities within commuting distance of most citizens, a commitment to flexibility, and, a commitment to the belief that quality and open access are compatible goals.

Misunderstandings of Open Access

Probably no single thing has been more troublesome to the community college than has been the use and abuse of the term, *the open door*. Many guidance counselors, high school teachers, college professors, and the public in general fail to understand that open access does not mean that anyone who meets the general admission requirements (a high school graduate or eighteen years of age or older) and can profit from attending can enroll in any program offered by the community college. Community college transfer programs have admission requirements almost identical to the requirements at most four-year institutions. Indeed, in almost all instances transfer programs offered at community colleges are patterned after senior institutions, even to the extent of identical course numbering. Technical programs in community colleges, nursing for example, have admission requirements at least as stringent as those for similar programs in other institutions. Yet the term, the open door, has so much appeal that it is almost irresistible: the term is catchy, easily remembered, appeals to a broad audience, is seemingly easily understood and almost universally identified with its sponsor, the community college. The term, had it been invented by Madison Avenue, would be considered a tour de force in the world of advertising.

If used carefully, the term *open door* can be a useful metaphor for community colleges' commitment to open access. Let us accept the concept that the community college does have a big open door through which everyone who has a key may pass. Keys are readily available to anyone who can meet the general admission requirements to the college; however, all keys are not alike. For example, an individual enters the open door of the community college, walks down the hallway, and comes to a door with a sign on it saying liberal arts. Taking the same key that opened the college's open door, the prospective student attempts to open the door to the room containing liberal arts. The door will not open, however. It will not open because the key does not have the notches and grooves that are created by having two units of college preparatory mathematics, a year of laboratory science, two years of a foreign language, four years of high school English, and other courses required to enter the liberal arts curriculum. The prospective student goes to the next door that has a sign, nursing. Again, the key will not open the door because certain prerequisites are missing. Rather than walking out of the college, which would likely happen if the individual were not in an open access institution, the prospective student decides to attempt to open the door labeled guidance and counseling. Here it is discovered that the same key that opened the main door to the college now opens the door to guidance and counseling. Once inside the counseling office, the student who has now completed the application to college, is given some choices. A number of doors can now be entered, for it is discovered that the key is, after all, versatile. One door that can be opened is the one labeled automobile mechanics, for example. Or the student may choose to have the key rekeyed by entering the door labeled developmental education. There it is learned that by taking developmental courses one can get those prerequisites added to the key and this will permit the student to open the door to liberal arts or to any other program offered by the college. Open access for this student and for other students means the opportunity to enter the wide open door, enter a program for which they are qualified, or to take courses that will prepare them to enter programs that they are currently unprepared to enter. Open access means that students other than only college-prep students will be accepted; however, open access does not mean admitting students to programs for which they are academically unprepared.

Criticisms of Open Access

A major criticism of open access community colleges is that many of the curriculums result in dead end jobs and that they lower rather than raise student aspirations. The most severe critics are those who argue that the community college is at the bottom of a hierarchical system of higher education, and, since minorities and other members of the lower socioeconomic class are more likely to attend the community college than they are to attend a four-year institution, the community college promotes social stratification by preserving the status quo and promotes educational inflation by requiring two years of education beyond high school in order to retain one's relative position in society. The most convincing argument in this genre is offered by Jerome Karabel (1972) who wrote, "... the community college, generally viewed as the leading edge of an open and egalitarian system of higher education, is in reality a prime expression of the dual historical patterns of class-based tracking and educational inflation" (p. 526).

A softer form of criticism is offered by those critics who accuse community colleges of "cooling out" students by lowering their aspirations from obtaining a bachelor's degree to settling for terminal occupational-technical programs offered at the community college. This thesis was developed and popularized by Burton Clark (1960, 1980), who concludes that some agency must be responsible for bringing students' aspirations into line with their abilities. Clark believes that cooling out is preferred over other alternatives (failing the student, for example) and concludes that the community college performs a valuable social function, and performs it well, through cooling out students.

The social critics have lost some of their sting as a result of the changing labor market; certain of the newer technical fields have become more attractive while some fields requiring the bachelor's degree, teaching for example, have lost social prestige and glamour. Community colleges should be sensitive to the tracking charge, however, especially as it pertains to class-based tracking.

Ten Ways to Close the Open Door

In order for the community college to fulfill its role successfully, certain conditions must exist. Taking the negative view, what would one do if one wants to destroy the effectiveness of an open access institution? The following activities and actions taken together are almost guaranteed to do the job.

1. Eliminate the comprehensive curriculum and concentrate solely on occupational-technical education or solely on the transfer function.

2. Eliminate developmental education and accept only those students who are prepared to do college level work.

3. Raise tuition to a level that prevents most members of the lower socioeconomic groups from attending college.

4. Eliminate or severely cut back on student financial aid, especially at the federal level.

5. Raise admission standards to a level that will assure that only those students who are among the academically talented and academically well prepared will be admitted. If academically weak students are admitted, make sure that their enrollment is limited to vocational programs.

6. Define quality in terms of the state university or in terms of the highly selective private college or university, thereby ignoring the community college's mission and philosophy and admitting that quality cannot exist in developmental education, in technical education, in community services courses, or in occupational education.

7. Ignore quality by lowering standards and thereby ensuring that all students, regardless of academic preparation, can enter and "successfully" complete all programs.

8. Ignore the station in life of students and promote the survival-of-the-fittest, sink-or-swim philosophy, a philosophy that gives the middle and upper classes a decided advantage. If members of the lower socioeconomic groups are admitted, place them in vocational programs, thereby providing more ammunition for social critics.

9. Cling to the notion popular during the 1960s that the community college can and should be all things to all people.

10. Most important, fail to articulate and interpret the community college's role to legislators, parents, students, and the public in general. This will guarantee that the mission is misunderstood and will result in the loss of public support, including funding.

While most community colleges have been guilty at one time or another of one or more of the above negative approaches to maintaining open access, none of the ten are compatible with the open access institution.

Why Preserve Open Access?

America's brand of democracy is founded on the belief that all people have the right and deserve the opportunity to achieve. This dream of equality has been reflected in the nation's comprehensive system of free or inexpensive public education. Moreover, through education, tax consumers can become tax producers; through education citizens will work for fair laws, honest government, and an economic and social system that is compatible with American democracy; through education, the nation will be able to compete in world markets while maintaining an adequate system of national defense; and, through education the individual achieves self-actualization.

While it is conceivable that open access to higher education could be achieved through other avenues, at the present time the comprehensive public community college is the nation's major avenue for educational advancement beyond high school for members of the lower socioeconomic groups, for older adults (especially women), for minorities, and for others who have been unable to achieve the American dream. Recognizing the value of educational opportunity beyond high school and recognizing the vital role the community college plays in providing educational opportunity, how can open access be maintained?

Maintaining Open Access

What can community college leaders do to help assure that the nation's commitment to open access to higher education does not become a victim of the conservative trends that are currently permeating the national mood? Much of the action should center around correcting or preventing the ten door-closing activities described above. The issues are complex and some are long standing; however, the complexity of the issues must not prevent community college leaders from taking action that can help assure that the community college remains the major vehicle for promoting open access at the post-high school level. What steps can be taken to assure that open access is maintained and that the integrity of the community college mission is not compromised?

The umbrella under which actions must take place if they are to be successful is that of interpreting the community college mission to its various publics consistently and accurately. All other activities revolve around how the mission is interpreted. Each of the remaining nine actions guaranteed to help close the open door will now be examined in light of how the mission is interpreted.

Comprehensiveness. Community college leaders must realize the importance of retaining program comprehensiveness. For example, during the 1960s occupational-technical education gained hegemony in many community colleges. The victim was often the college transfer function. A healthy transfer curriculum must be maintained, for the bachelor's degree remains the steppingstone for entering positions of leadership and for entering the professions. During the lifelong learning boom of the 1970s, the community college program was often not coherent. The mission became fuzzy; often community college leaders failed to understand the nature of what was happening to the community college and legislators and the public failed to understand the broadened mission. To revert to the junior college of the early part of the century would be a mistake, however. Occupational-technical education has an important role to play in the comprehensive curriculum as do community services offerings; however, neither should be allowed to crowd out the transfer mission. If integrity is to be maintained, the mission must remain comprehensive.

Developmental Education. An important component of the comprehensive mission is developmental education. However, legislators in a number of states are increasingly hesitant to fund developmental education at the post-high school level. Why, they are asking, should taxpayers pay twice for the same education? The question is legitimate and community college leaders have an obligation to provide answers, especially if they expect funding for developmental education. For example, most community colleges admit anyone who is eighteen years of age or older who can benefit from attending college. Yet most colleges have failed to define the ability to benefit in academic terms. It must be remembered that the purpose of developmental education is to prepare individuals to enter a college curriculum, not to provide an avenue for generating student credit hours for the institution or to provide a stopping place for students on financial aid. Legislators and the public must be made aware of the many older adults who, for whatever reason, cannot succeed in college without first taking developmental courses. For example, a number of mature women who enter the community college's nursing program must have developmental chemistry before being admitted to the program. This fact must be articulated. Indeed, regardless of their educational level most adults would need developmental courses in the sciences, mathematics, and any subject requiring extensive use of computers were they to return to college. Yet the only thing legislators know about the developmental program in many cases is that the community college is teaching high school graduates reading, writing, and arithmetic. The other purposes of developmental education must be articulated by community college leaders; at the same time, leaders need to define and understand the role of developmental education on their own campuses.

Tuition Rates. One of the characteristics of the open access institution is its relatively low cost to the individual. To raise tuition beyond the reach of a large number of individuals is to deny them access to the institution. In Virginia, for example, tuition has increased 108 percent since 1981. During this time period fulltime equivalent enrollment has declined 12 percent and black enrollment has declined 13 percent. While it is difficult to establish the correlation between college costs to the individual and college attendance, it nevertheless behooves community college leaders to let their state legislators know that there is a point at which the cost of attending college is prohibitive for those segments of society that need it most and to let them know that when costs to the individual reach a certain level, open access has gone down the drain both figuratively and literally.

Student Financial Aid. If, as suggested earlier, the nation's commitment to providing open access to higher education depends to a large part on federal student aid, then it follows that continued cutbacks in federal student aid will move the nation away from this commitment. For example, the American Association of State Colleges and Universities recently reported that, although more blacks and Hispanics are graduating from high school, the percentage going to college is declining. Without federal financial aid, many students will simply be squeezed out of higher education, especially if federal student financial aid fails to keep up with rising tuition rates, a situation that has existed the past few years.

Quality. Quality is a relative term and must be defined in relative terms. Community college leaders must not succumb to the temptation to view quality as a transportable item but rather must realize that quality exists in developmental programs, technical programs, and student services, as well as in the more traditional programs associated with higher education. Quality then, must be defined in terms of the community college's philosophy and mission. This definition must be compatible with the definition of open access and quality must not be used as an excuse to exclude those students the open access institution is designed to serve.

Admission Standards. One approach to improving quality is to raise admission standards, an approach that is unacceptable to community colleges. Indeed, community colleges must resist the temptation to raise admission standards as a means of improving quality. Open access means that admission standards are inclusive rather than exclusive. On the other hand, community college leaders must be very sensitive to see that admission standards are not confused with exit standards. That is, the student who enters the nursing program with a relatively weak background in chemistry must not be allowed to graduate with a weak background in anything.

Family Background. Should community colleges admit students who, because of their station in life are not prepared for college academically and, in some cases, socially? Most community college leaders would respond very quickly that, "Of course, they should be admitted." When pressed, however, the answer might be, "Yes, they should be admitted, but only to those programs for which they are qualified." That answer is not good enough. The open access institution must take some chances on the student's ability to succeed and provide the necessary support services such as counseling, academic advising, and financial assistance, thereby increasing the student's chances of success, especially for those students who are members of lower socioeconomic groups. The community college must become an equal opportunity college for students as well as for employees.

"All Things to All People." One of the places the mission went astray was when community college leaders decided that the role of the community college was to eliminate poverty, correct environmental ills, find suitable housing for the ill-housed, and do other things that often went well beyond the scope of the teaching and learning process. As most community college leaders are discovering, community colleges do not have the financial, physical, or intellectual resources to be all things to all people. Nor do they have a public mandate to perform those functions for which they receive no funding and that go well beyond their mission. Once these things are realized by its leaders, the community college can settle down to deciding what it can and should be doing as an institution of higher education.

Summary

In summary, if the community college is to maintain its integrity, it must be true to its mission and to its philosophy, and it must articulate that philosophy and mission to its constituents in an effective and consistent manner. Maintaining integrity means drawing some boundaries in regard to its mission and philosophy. Its mission, above all else, must be built on offering a comprehensive program; its philosphy, above all else, must be built on open access. To compromise these aspects of its mission or philosophy is to compromise its integrity, a position no open-access institution can afford to assume if it hopes to achieve its potential in helping to fulfill the American dream.

References

Clark, B. R. "The 'Cooling-Out' Function in Higher Education." *The American Journal of Sociology*, 1960, *65* (6), 569–576.

Clark, B. R. "The 'Cooling Out' Function Revisited." In G. B. Vaughan (Ed.), *Questioning the Community College Role*. New Directions for Community Colleges, no. 32. San Francisco: Jossey-Bass, 1980.

Karabel, J. "Community Colleges and Social Stratification." *Harvard Educational Review*, 1972, *42* (4), 521–562.

George B. Vaughan is president of Piedmont Virginia Community College and author of numerous articles and books on the community college.

Threats to institutional integrity can come from within or without. Major threats are the avoidance of difficult management decisions and the failure to control and direct change.

General Threats to Institutional Integrity

Gordon K. Davies

Institutions may be damaged not just from the outside but from within as well. One of the greatest threats to institutions today is avoidance of difficult management decisions. We are in a time of rapid change, and college administrators will hurt their institutions if they let them drift with the current.

Threats from without cannot be measured precisely, much less defined. What is a threat from one perspective (the president's) may be an expression of popular demand for change from another (a legislator's). My impression, based on reading, listening, and personal experience, is that external intrusion into the workings of American colleges and universities was much higher in the decades before and immediately after World War II than it is today. By intrusion, I mean ideological pressure on the curriculum, interference in staff appointments, favoritism in awarding contracts, and the like.

Intrusion from Business

Intrusion today seems to be more subtle and ambiguous. Colleges and universities are in danger of becoming subservient to business interests, for instance, for a number of reasons. First, we live in a high fashion culture, and what is fashionable now is the business-education partnership. The surest way into the taxpayer's pocket is to speak with passionate intensity about education's role in economic development and high technology. This is a common illusion that may have damaging effects on colleges and universities if pushed too far.

Second, as competition for state revenues becomes more fierce and as the federal government withdraws support for higher education, colleges and universities are turning to business as a potential source of support. This support can come as contributions of money and equipment, as special purchase arrangements for equipment, as funding for applied research, or through formal partnerships that take advantage of federal tax law provisions for private investors. The effect of these relationships on the integrity of colleges and universities is a matter of concern to those who care about higher education. This is not to say that the relationships are bad in themselves. But they pose a definite threat that should be acknowledged.

Third, it has been the "propaganda" for many years that a college education is the way to get a good job and move up the social and economic ladder. Students have bought this pitch, and the numbers of majors in business and other professional programs threaten to overbalance the curriculum. Institutions that were colleges of the arts and sciences have become schools of professional studies. Some teacher education colleges have been transformed by student demand into business colleges without ever having developed a coherent undergraduate curriculum in the arts and sciences.

There may now be a reaction beginning against the notion that the curriculum should be shaped by student demand. If so, it is a good sign. But we should be aware that the reaction, if there really is one, was not started by college faculty and administrators. Reform is being pressed on higher education from without. This in itself is an ironic commentary on the complaints of institutional personnel about unwarranted intrusion into their affairs. Intrusion is a matter of perception.

Intrusion from the State

Intrusion can come from the state level, either from state agencies or from the central office of a higher education system. State management systems for accounting, personnel, and procurement, for instance, often require that individual record processing done by institutions be replicated at a higher level. Such redundancy can be deadening to campus administrators, who see their work delayed, questioned, or overruled by persons who have no direct responsibility for institutional management.

State policies and, even worse, state systems and procedures can force changes in the organization, curriculum, and pedagogy of colleges and universities. For instance, employment ceilings can create pressure to use more parttime faculty. Up to a point, and the point will differ for each institution, parttime faculty are a valuable asset. Beyond that point, however, the core of fulltime faculty becomes too small to carry out the nonteaching responsibilities of faculty: curriculum planning and review, advising, library acquisition review, general committee work, and more. In addition, the manner in which teaching is performed can be limited by large numbers of parttime faculty. They make it difficult to maintain a tightly organized academic program in which courses complement one another.

Virginia's state coordinating agency, the State Council of Higher Education for Virginia (SCHEV), has statutory responsibility to review the productivity of academic programs and require that nonproductive programs be discontinued. The primary criterion that has been employed for almost a decade has been degrees conferred, followed by enrollments, and then by other factors, such as unusually strongly sponsored research or public service activities.

We who are responsible for SCHEV policies realized last year, as a result of a major conference on reform of the undergraduate curriculum sponsored by the agency, that the productivity review criteria and procedures were affecting curriculum decisions on some campuses in ways inconsistent with the Council's broader interests. The Council was urging, for instance, that college graduates have competence in a foreign language, and be familiar with English literature. It was not insisting that more students major in foreign languages or English literature, as the review criteria would seem to indicate.

However, using degrees conferred as the primary criterion of productivity was creating the wrong impression and was causing faculties to contort the curriculum in bizarre ways. The Council is revising the criteria and procedures as a result, and one revision will be to remove primary emphasis on degrees conferred.

State level policies and management systems also can intrude on institutions by providing incentives to operate in ways that are wasteful in the long run. For instance, it is generally agreed that it is better to buy with public money the things an institution needs most, rather than the things it can afford in any one budget period. But most government budget policies require that unspent money revert to the general fund at the end of every budget period. The money an institution returns is presumed to be money it did not need, and often the next appropriation is reduced by that amount.

Since an administration cannot save money over several years to purchase a needed piece of equipment and since it stands to lose money in the next budget if it gives any back from the previous one, there is a clear incentive to spend all the money appropriated, even if it is spent on lower priority purchases. Some critics call this bad management, but it is not. Within the budget system, it is very good manangement. However, it is a bad system, and it leads to actions that are contrary to the public good.

Another general principle on which there is agreement is that public agencies and institutions should pay their bills when they are due. Paying them earlier than their due dates reduces the investment yields on an institution's money. Paying them later may lead to penalties and inconveniences for vendors who do business with the state.

But if they do not retain the investment yields on their cash reserves and if the yields become part of the state general fund even when a substantial portion of the cash reserve derives from tuition and fees, institutions have little incentive to pay their bills on time. A college or university administration well might choose to pay its bills on a schedule convenient to its computer center administration rather than attempting to get the greatest possible investment yield on its money.

Bureaucracy need not be designed by Kafka in order to have deadening effects on the human spirit. It need not be run by incompetent or malicious people in order to dissociate responsibility from authority. Redundancy is redundancy, no matter how well-intentioned, and it is deadening to the spirit.

There are signs that several state governments are seeking to change their relationships with colleges and universities. In general, these states have focused efforts on decentralizing selected administrative activities. While no state has entirely decentralized, several have made a start. Kentucky has taken the most comprehensive approach toward new forms of management. Wisconsin started with a broad evaluation and acted on specific problems. Maryland started with a review of governance and, while not reaching agreement on a different system, nonetheless acted on some specific problems. State government action in Colorado, Idaho, Connecticut, Massachusetts and Washington have been partial. Virginia is developing plans for limited decentralization of fiscal and accounting, procurement and personnel practices. New Jersey is considering legislation to give its state colleges more operational freedom.

The degree of management autonomy afforded higher education in the states does not appear to be related to the perceived national stature of their colleges and universities. A study by J. Fredericks Volkwein (1984) attempted to document and quantify the degree of state control over higher education administrative practices. Volkwein analyzed controls in forty-nine states (Alaska was excluded) as they affected eighty-eight doctoral institutions. A "flexibility/control index" was developed to rate the degree of flexibility in fiscal and administrative matters, and the states were ranked accordingly.

States whose major universities have outstanding reputations were scattered throughout the list. North Carolina ranked forty-seventh, Wisconsin thirty-third, California twenty-fifth, and Michigan fifth. While administrative flexibility might be desirable for other reasons, Volkwein's index seems to indicate that it is not a necessary condition for excellence in higher education.

State Protection of Integrity

State bureaucracy poses a danger to institutional integrity when it inhibits the ability of colleges and universities to change with the times. Change is difficult for any institution, whether it be a government agency or a university. State government can preserve integrity best and threaten it least when it provides colleges and universities with access to modern management and financial techniques and to modern equipment with which to fulfill their missions. Consider two examples.

Alternative Financing Techniques. The funding pattern of state supported higher education has changed gradually over the past twenty years and is changing now at an accelerated rate. State and federal support is more limited, and tuition has been increased without corresponding increases in financial assistance for needy students. Expenditures have been reduced, usually in the areas of equipment and plant maintenance. Higher education is now in a situation in which the problems of accumulated equipment deficiencies and aging physical plants cannot be solved with general fund tax dollars and tuition and fees alone. The needs are too great and these traditional sources of funding are too limited.

Colleges and universities need access to alternative sources of revenue in order to maintain their current missions. For instance, several methods of raising funds for equipment acquisition have been used, each of which extends payment over the useful life of the equipment, offers an economic advantage to the provider of the funds, or uses the tax laws and the exempt status of colleges and universities to reduce the cost of debt.

Among these methods are the issuance of debt, either long-term or short-term, to spread the costs of acquisition over a greater number of annual budgets. Alternatively, private enterprise may realize greater tax advantages by donating scientific equipment for research or research training. They also may earn tax credit for research expenditures as members of limited partnerships with research universities.

Another method of raising funds for equipment is to transfer a depreciable asset (such as a hospital) from a state university to private ownership, thereby allowing private enterprise to take the investment tax credit and depreciation allowances. The institution continues to use the asset at a reasonable lease price while having use of the cash from the sale.

Funding methods such as those described above require a new relationship between state agencies and institutions of higher education. For one thing, the cost of issuing debt can be greatly reduced if it is done as a pooled effort on behalf of all institutions. The origination costs of the debt instrument (bond counsel, banking, insurance, rating) preclude smaller institutions from going it alone and limit the capacity of larger ones. A state agency or authority should be empowered to perform this function for higher education.

Second, issues such as intellectual property rights (patents, copyrights, and the like) have to be understood clearly before joint research efforts with private enterprise are undertaken. Finally, the sale and leaseback of depreciable assets is attractive only if the cash from the sale is dedicated to meeting higher education needs.

State governments must develop the capacity that most do not have today to encourage alternative ways of financing higher education. Most attorneys in general do not have the staff to provide counsel as states plan debt issues for higher education equipment. They have little capacity to advise colleges and universities about opportunities created by federal or state tax law. Most state treasurers are not used to dealing with short-term debt because most state debt is long-term and fixed-rate.

State government must relax some forms of control and develop new ones. Institutions or higher education systems should have greater control over cash generated by sale of assets, as tuition, from other revenue, or from management efficiencies. At the same time, controls should be established to ensure that debt is justified by the needs of higher education and not by the demands of the financial institutions that profit by issuing them. Controls are needed to ensure that sale-leaseback arrangements, limited research partnerships, and other revenue producing activities do not distract institutions from their designated missions. The emphasis should be on developing capacities and controls that are appropriate to the anticipated financial situation of higher education over the next several years.

Telecommunications Networks. No single institution is capable of taking full advantage of the educational capacity of modern telecommunications. As the size and characteristics of the population change, and as the demand for educational opportunities becomes more extensive, state governments can and should make communications networks available for educational purposes.

The population of a state may decline, especially in the traditional college age group, but neither the diversity nor the intensity of demands for higher education will diminish proportionately. Indeed, even if there are fewer young men and women graduating from secondary schools, the notion that higher education should be accessible throughout a state will remain, and so will the political pressure to make education available to the people.

Telecommunications networks with the capacity to support computer-assisted and televised instruction should be a component of every state's higher education system. Providing instruction over long distances can increase faculty productivity in some programs and disciplines, thereby relieving pressure on the institution as a whole. With a telecommunications network in place, instruction can be provided when and where it is needed. Perhaps as important, it can be stopped when and where it no longer is needed. This flexibility is no small advantage when compared to the alternative expenses of providing instructors on site throughout a state.

The mobility afforded by telecommunications is especially attractive to states whose major universities are not located close to major urban industrial centers. These states, and there are probably more in this situation than not, are constantly under pressure to duplicate the capacities of their sister universities in the urban centers. Developing a telecommunications network for instruction allows those responsible for higher education planning to meet needs without duplicating programs over the state.

In the long run, sophisticated telecommunications will allow states to exchange instructional programs, thus creating regional and national delivery systems that make state borders irrelevant to higher education. While this possibility threatens some established interests, it is consistent with the kind of social and commercial intercourse that characterizes our mobile and technologically sophisticated society.

Community college systems, with their mission to provide education within commuting distance of those who want and can benefit from it, can make great use of telecommunications. Because of their mission, community colleges often are located in sparsely populated areas and lack the enrollment base needed to sustain comprehensive curricula. Computer-assisted or televised instruction (with two-way voice communication) can augment the local capacity at lesser cost than providing faculty at each site.

Technical programs also can be augmented by broadcasts orginating from larger community colleges. Programs can be sent to a location and easily discontinued when the demand for them has been met. It is far easier to switch off a computer or television set than it is to move faculty or to close buildings.

States should develop telecommunications networks. They will reduce costs in the long run, help to solve political problems, and increase the range and quality of services a state can afford to provide. They also will help institutions maintain their academic integrity by enabling them to provide better programs than they could otherwise offer.

Reference

Volkwein, J. F. "State Financial Control Practices and Public Univerities: Results of a National Study." Paper presented at the annual meeting of the Association for the Study of Higher Education, Chicago, March 1984.

Gordon K. Davies is the director of the State Council of Higher Education for Virginia.

Whether a faculty member is full- or parttime may be irrelevant to the question of the impact of all faculty members on institutional or academic integrity.

Parttime Faculty: Integrity and Integration

Judith L. McGaughey

Parttime faculty have become an important and regular feature of the community college. In 1966, parttime faculty comprised 23 percent of all college teachers, by 1980 the figure had risen to 41 percent. According to statistics from the American Association of Community and Junior Colleges (AACJC), parttime faculty comprise more than half (55.8 percent) of all faculty in two-year colleges (Leslie, Kellams, and Gunne, 1982).

The National Center for Education Statistics (NCES) estimates that one in every three faculty is employed parttime—more than 250,000 individuals. It is further estimated that parttime faculty provide at least 15 percent of all instruction (Gappa, 1984). This proportion is even higher in community colleges, the primary employer of parttime faculty.

Although there is not a standard definition of parttime, there is general agreement that it refers to less than a fulltime commitment in any institution. With regard to faculty, it usually refers to any appointment that encompasses less than a normal range of assigned duties and in which the terms of employment recognize the fractional involvement of the faculty member (Leslie, Kellams, and Gunne, 1982).

In converting the notion of parttime to a fulltime equivalent

D. Puyear (Ed.). *Maintaining Institutional Integrity.* New Directions for Community Colleges, no. 52. San Francisco: Jossey-Bass, December 1985.

(FTE) base, the National Center for Education Statistics assumes that parttime employment represents one-third of an FTE. They further estimate that, across all institutions of higher education, about 20 percent of all instruction is done by parttime faculty. In community colleges, the figure is probably closer to 30 percent.

Growth projections of parttime faculty are mixed. Leslie, Kellams, and Gunne (1982) believe that the number of parttime faculty members will increase. They attribute this to the projected growth of nontraditional college populations (for example, older women, off-campus students, career changers), populations typically served by parttime faculty. This will occur at the same time that the traditional, college age cohort number will decline.

As Eliason points out (Parsons, 1980), the adult learner will be the largest single growth population throughout the 1980s. The adult who turns to the community college for new skills and credentials is likely to expect immediate service. Colleges must be ready to provide educational opportunities that are responsive to changing job requirements. A static, tenured faculty may not be able to adequately respond to the fast paced changes of student demand and the marketplace.

Rationales for Use of Parttime Faculty

Typically, three factors support the rationale for using parttime faculty in the community college:
1. It is less costly to hire parttime faculty than to hire fulltime faculty.
2. Community colleges need flexibility in responding to the fast changing student marketplace. Parttime faculty allow for institutional flexibility to a greater degree than do fulltime faculty.
3. Rapidly changing technology requires faculty with expertise in new fields. Parttime faculty drawn from science and industry are more likely to have the expertise new technologies demand.

The cost saving feature of parttime faculty should not be a primary rationale for hiring. Typically, the parttime faculty member is paid less (an hourly or course rate rather than an annual salary) and does not have a full range of accompanying fringe benefits (as does the fulltime faculty member). Additionally, he or she usually receives a less secure hiring commitment from the institution; per course, pending sufficient enrollment or as a substitute for a fulltime faculty member are likely to be conditions of such employment.

In spite of these economical features (from the administrator's perspective), effective institutional responses to assure quality instruction usually require additional resources directed at the parttime faculty member. Such resources may include: additional administrators to ensure consistent hiring practices, compensation to administrators or faculty to regularly supervise and evaluate parttime faculty, and financial support of professional development activities for parttime faculty. The provision of these resources may become key factors in the parttime faculty member's potential for success in the classroom.

It is usually true that community colleges can be more quickly responsive to rapidly changing student and market demands by hiring parttime faculty. The flexibility to quickly match surges or declines in student population with parttime faculty hirings or firings is a fact of educational economics that cannot be ignored. But since this flexibility creates a rather insecure environment for the parttime faculty member, it should not be viewed only as positive. It behooves the institution to create ways to be responsive to changing conditions through the use of both full- and parttime faculty. Such strategies may include hiring faculty with qualifications to teach in more than one discipline, subsidizing retraining for fulltime faculty in emerging fields, and providing other professional opportunities for faculty such as occasional special teaching or administrative assignments.

In short, it seems likely that the strongest institutions will be those able to mobilize both full- and parttime faculty to be effective and knowledgeable responders to new fields, new student populations, and new programmatic thrusts.

It may be helpful to now look at parttime faculty in the context of institutional integrity. This author suggests four major factors that indicate the degree of institutional integrity that exists in a community college: (1) adequacy of facilities and equipment, (2) adequacy of institutional funding, (3) academic integrity and quality of instruction, (4) reputational factors—quality of students, innovativeness, special attributes of the institution (for example, core curriculum, specialized programs, publications, special services).

These attributes will exist in varying degrees in an institution regardless of the mix of full- and parttime faculty. For the purposes of this chapter, our focus will be on the third factor, academic integrity or the quality of instruction. What is the relationship of parttime faculty to this attribute?

Parttime Faculty: Recruitment and Selection

It can be inferred that the quality of instruction will at least be partially dependent on the quality of the faculty providing instruction. In order to ensure the hiring of qualified parttime faculty, an adequate and consistent faculty recruitment and hiring process should be established. Administrators should not depend on "friend of a friend" or "day-before-classes" hiring or on overload assignments for fulltime faculty. In each of these instances the necessary expertise, experience, or commitment of the faculty member thus selected may be jeopardized. As Harris points out (Parsons, 1980), colleges should develop a systematic, rational, and continuous program for parttime faculty recruitment. The creation of an ongoing pool of potential parttime faculty can help ensure that faculty ultimately selected will be qualified and committed. It is far more possible to create a potential pool of parttime faculty to draw on in the future than to do so with fulltime faculty, since their need for primary employment is usually immediate. Such parttime faculty pools should be developed and maintained.

Gappa (1984) points out that parttime faculty are usually recruited from the local labor market. In urban areas, this may pose less of a problem in selecting qualified personnel since the potential available pool of personnel is likely to be larger. In less urban areas, colleges may need to be more creative in attracting parttime faculty from further distances (paying for carfare) or hiring for short term incentives (perhaps offering short term stays in dormitories or in the homes of fulltime faculty).

As with fulltime faculty, parttime faculty should be interviewed by department chairpersons, program directors, or appropriate faculty. References should be checked and, ideally, the parttime faculty member should be observed teaching (even in simulation) prior to hiring.

What about credentials? Research to date suggests that most parttime faculty are less credentialed than fulltime faculty. A 1972-1973 ACE survey of fulltime faculty reports that 45 percent have master's degrees and 41 percent have a doctorate or professional degree, compared to 40 percent and 20 percent respectively for parttime faculty (Tuckman, 1981). This may not mean that parttime faculty are less qualified to teach. Parttime faculty often bring different skills to their work that may not be related to their degrees—both in terms of field of study and level of attainment. Richard Ernst and Larry McFarlane, in a 1977 study of faculty at North Virginia Community College, reviewed the credentials of 800 parttime faculty and discovered academic preparation to be equal (Leslie, 1978). Although they do not indicate the specific levels of equal preparation, they do point out that the Virginia State Board for Community Colleges has established identical employment criteria for both fulltime and parttime faculty (Leslie, 1978). More research needs to be done in this area to correlate faculty credentials with quality of instruction and instructional outputs (performance of students). Gappa (1984) postulates that with the decline in the availability of fulltime, tenure track faculty positions (because of projected enrollment declines), many new Ph.D.s will seek other careers but may also desire a parttime teaching affiliation in higher education.

Parttime Faculty and Quality of Instruction

An issue of occasional debate centers on whether parttime faculty detract from or enhance the quality of instruction in an institution. Data can be found to support proponents of both views. This author contends that the status of the faculty member (part- or fulltime) is not the key variable in the debate. What is more important is the faculty member's knowledge base, communication ability, and his or her commitment to and motivations for teaching.

As Gappa (1984) points out, educational preparation and scholarly activity cannot be viewed as the only indicators of quality in a comparison of parttime and fulltime faculty. Parttime faculty (for example, musicians, architects, chefs, accountants) represent a wide range of skills, experience, and expertise. Those who hold fulltime positions elsewhere will ideally bring their experience to enrich their teaching. This integration of learning with life/work experience may be especially effective for the more mature, nontraditional student who also brings a range of work and life experience to the classroom.

In an analysis of data collected by James Bess in his 1976 and 1977 studies of faculty role/activity preferences, Kellams and Kyre (Leslie, 1978) discovered that the distribution of goal preferences of parttime faculty is more variable than for fulltime faculty. At the same time, fulltime faculty hold more homogeneous educational values. Part of this may stem from the fact that a significant proportion of fulltime faculty have come from a middle class strata that engenders similar values (for example, places importance on the value of education, espouses deferred gratification, believes in the traditional societal structures and strictures).

Kellams and Kyre point out striking differences in preferences between the two groups. Parttime faculty appear to prefer more nontraditional instructional activities, like to work in a more interdisciplinary, collaborative mode, and prefer service and writing activities that are less academic in nature. They go on to say that parttime faculty seem more likely to fit into colleges and universities where innovative instruction is encouraged and where community and student based activities are supported (Leslie, 1978). This has important implications as community colleges look to the growth potential of various nontraditional student populations. Such populations may have needs and interests that will require new curricular, locational, and scheduling models. Parttime faculty may be among those most suitable to meet these changing dimensions.

If motivational factors can be linked to parttime faculty's teaching effectiveness, recent research by Leslie, Kellams, and Gunne (1982) is interesting. They gathered data on work histories and career aspirations from 104 parttime faculty at fourteen colleges. They discovered that the leading motive for teaching parttime was a matter of personal satisfaction. Teaching brought fulfillment and accomplishment. The second most frequent motivator was professional. These parttime faculty members had fulltime nonacademic careers. They saw the classroom as a place to apply their professional expertise while also stimulating students to look beyond the academic and theoretical frameworks of learning. The third motivator was career aspiration—parttime faculty who wanted fulltime positions but were unsuccessful in this goal. Although not successful in obtaining fulltime employment, many accepted parttime teaching assignments as a potential route to a future fulltime teaching career. The least frequent motivator was economic. While the extra money was helpful, it was not the primary reason for teaching (Gappa, 1984).

It should not be surprising that economic motivation is not primary. It is no secret that salaries paid to full- and parttime faculty have generally eroded in relation to salaries paid to other professionals. More often than not in conversations with full- and parttime faculty, they will state that the work they do is worth more than what they are paid. This may be especially true for the outstanding teacher who regularly spends many hours in teaching preparation and in extra work with students. Also, in the instance of parttime faculty, not an insignificant part of their pay may go toward the cost of travel to and from off campus teaching locations or from one parttime teaching assignment to another in a different institution. Many faculty members lament the diminution in status of teaching as a profession and believe that inadequate salaries play a significant part in this erosion.

Given the positive, noneconomic nature of the primary motivators (professional and intrinsic), it would be wise for community colleges to capitalize on these factors in their professional development efforts with parttime faculty.

Any discussion of parttime faculty should include reference to Friedlander's research comparing the quality of instruction between full- and parttime faculty. He identified eleven criteria that he deemed likely to affect the quality of instruction (Friedlander, 1979). In every dimension he discovered that parttime faculty had less or did less than fulltime faculty (for example, 90 percent of fulltimers had at least two year's teaching experience versus 65 percent for parttimers, 56 percent of fulltimers had say over classroom texts versus 11 percent of parttimers). Friedlander then goes on to say that, despite these differences in practices, there is no statistical evidence that students who enroll in courses taught by parttime faculty receive an inferior quality of instruction.

It is unfortunate that Friedlander did not attach weighted values to the eleven criteria since some of them seem more instrumental to effective teaching than others. It is possible to organize these criteria into three categories: primary, intermediate, and secondary. It is suggested that at the community college level, teaching experience and selection of course materials are primary criteria. The faculty's use of media and availability to students would be intermediate factors while the use of support services and involvement in professional activities would be secondary in relation to successful teaching. Again, there may be little relationship between these criteria, the parttime faculty member's performance in the classroom, and student outcomes.

Other studies of instructional effectiveness have, among other things, focused on students' ratings of teachers. A study of full- and parttime faculty at Elgin Community College in Illinois measured three variables: students' ratings of teachers' effectiveness, class retention rates, and subsequent student achievement in advanced courses (Gappa, 1984). No significant differences, across these three dimensions, between full- and parttime faculty were found.

In 1982, the author conducted a small study at LaGuardia Community College of the City University of New York using the Student Instructional Report (SIR), published by the Educational Testing Service. As only one measure of teaching effectiveness, the form was used to determine any significant rating differences between full- and parttime faculty.

An analysis of student responses to various items on the SIR for twenty-eight faculty members (fourteen fulltime and fourteen parttime) yielded the following results: (1) Fulltime faculty seemed to be somewhat more successful than parttime faculty in stimulating students to think for themselves; (2) parttime faculty had slightly higher mean scores than fulltime faculty on instructor preparedness and overall quality of instruction. Because of the extremely small size of the sample, it is difficult to know if these outcomes are statistically significant but they do provide food for thought. Given the limitations of student ratings and the subjective nature of classifying elements of effective instruction it is crucial that any analysis of ratings be done with care and that conclusions be considered tentative at best. In spite of this, we again have data that suggest fulltime and parttime faculty can be equally effective, though in different dimensions.

Although the information available comparing teaching effectiveness of parttime and fulltime faculty is inconclusive, it appears that parttime faculty do not detract from the quality of instruction and may, indeed, enrich it. As suggested by Leslie, Kellams, and Gunne (1982), key factors seem to be how parttime faculty are selected, supported, and assigned.

Parttime Faculty and the Institution

It would seem important for institutional integrity that parttime faculty be integrated into the life of the community college to the fullest extent possible. Orientation to the institution including its philosophy, facilities, programs, and the nature of its student body needs to be accomplished. There are varying ways to do this. With the increasing number of home video cassette players, it may be possible to put orientations on videotape for the parttime faculty members to view at home at their convenience prior to the beginning of the semester. Departmental meetings and faculty handbooks are other orientation sources.

Although it is not usually feasible for parttime faculty to have their own offices, community colleges need to be more resourceful and creative in providing work space for adjunct faculty. It should not be inconceivable for a fulltime day faculty member to share his or her office with a parttime evening faculty member. The college might make a few offices available to parttime faculty who could share them based on different teaching schedules. This may not be possible within a department, but across the institution, schedules may vary enough to make such arrangements feasible. Also, the copy machine must be available and in working order day and night. A resource room, shared by several departments, might be created for parttime faculty. It should have work space, phones, typewriters, and copy machines accessible to parttime faculty.

All students should be exposed to both full- and parttime faculty.

Given the increasing diversity of our students, it seems likely that their learning can only be enriched by the diversity of full- and parttime faculty as long as that faculty is effectively prepared.

There are varying perspectives on what role parttime faculty should play in an institution's governance. Most studies indicate they play a minimal role. To the extent that governance deals with the perpetuation of a structure and with defining faculty roles external to the classroom, it may not be essential for parttime faculty to be actively involved in college governance. To the extent governance deals with issues of curriculum, teaching methodology, workload, and compensation, parttime faculty should be represented and involved.

One possible vehicle for representation would be to create a parttime faculty advisory council. Elected by their peers to the council, these faculty would act as peer representatives on various important college bodies — for example, senate, curriculum, personnel, and budget committees.

Effective integration must encompass professional development and skills enhancement opportunities for parttime faculty. Next to orientation to the institution and its students, parttime faculty most desire assistance with teaching strategies and diagnosing student levels and needs. In-service seminars pairing experienced faculty with new faculty to test out teaching approaches may be worthwhile. Video taping of parttime faculty teaching with opportunity for self-critique can be another valuable resource.

It is also essential that parttime faculty be evaluated. In whatever way fulltime faculty are evaluated (for example, student evaluations, peer observations, departmental review), a parallel system should exist for parttime faculty. There should also be promotional opportunities or work incentives for parttime faculty. In less rigid structures, this might take the form of merit bonuses or some other special recognition. In less flexible systems it might take the form of free dinners for parttime faculty professional development sessions, or of arrangements for parttime faculty to make presentations to other faculty groups. The latter notion has the potential for elevating the status and reputation of participating parttime faculty. As Gappa (1984) points out, the common features of successful development programs require: commitment of college leadership, a program based on an honest assessment of what parttime faculty believe is essential, incentives for faculty participation, and activities scheduled at convenient times (as difficult as that may be).

Summary

As has been suggested throughout this chapter, whether a faculty member is full- or parttime may not be the critical variable for institutional integrity. The wholeness of an institution and its academic program is, in the best settings, greater than the sum of its parts. If an institution has strong academic programs, this is often reflected in enduring commitment to excellence beyond monetary reward on the part of both full- and parttime faculty members.

The quality and diversity of parttime faculty and their primary motivations for teaching would suggest that they bring integrity to the institution. It is now up to the institution to assure, through its hiring, review, and development policies and procedures, that the parttime faculty member can be effectively integrated into the life of the college — especially its academic components.

Many educators regret the fact that there is tremendous variability in the uses and practices of parttime faculty, that there are no standard norms. Perhaps this is not so bad. Too often, as institutions attempt to institutionalize and firmly regulate conditions, such as the specific requirements of faculty involvement, they must also face a concomitant loss of flexibility and responsiveness. This is not to say parttime faculty do not have rights to be protected. The basic conditions for their employment and the expectations of employee and employer should be carefully spelled out and agreed on before hiring commitments are made.

These conditions and standards should be developed in the context of the particular college's needs and priorities with a view to both internal and external conditions. Since these conditions may vary tremendously from college to college, it may be counterproductive to create national or even regional norms or standards regulating parttime faculty involvement in higher education.

One of the thornier points seems to be the dichotomy, and occasional competitive or adversarial stance assumed, between the role and function of parttime faculty in contrast to that of fulltime faculty. Many legal decisions have supported this dichotomy and indicate that a sufficient community of interest does not exist between full- and parttime faculty — and thus they should be represented by different bargaining units.

It is time to diffuse this dichotomy. Faculty should have a variety of roles to play in the institution and these roles should be measured in both function and multiple-time segments. Faculty should choose what roles they desire and are capable of fulfilling, in concert with institutional needs and priorities. For example, the options could include teaching for x hours, student advisement for y hours, serving on committees for z hours and handling a special project (for example, curriculum/materials development) for m hours. Each category would have an hourly pay rate attached to it. One faculty member might select twelve hours of teaching and five hours of special project work. Another might select four hours of teaching and two of advisement. A third might select six hours of teaching, ten of student advisement, and three of committee work. Undoubtedly, some adjustments would need to be made to assure that faculty roles mesh with institutional goals.

Under such a plan, faculty would perform a multitude of teaching related functions (and be paid differentially for each) with some more than fulltime, some three-quarter time, some five-eighths time, some one-third time, and so forth.

Creating a system of differential pay for particular academic services offered in varying time frames would be similar to how other professionals (attorneys, doctors, accountants, for example) are recognized and compensated.

Although such a plan would be difficult to develop and might even be unwieldy initially, it might, in the long run, better serve institutional and student needs. It might also create the impetus for a true community of scholars and teachers who are valued or devalued based on the particular number of hours they teach.

References

Ernst, R. J. and McFarlane, L. A. "Are We Shortchanging Our Students by Using Parttime Faculty?" In D. W. Leslie (Ed.), *Employing Parttime Faculty*. New Directions for Institutional Research, no. 18. San Francisco: Jossey-Bass, 1978.

Friedlander, J. "Instructional Practices of Parttime and Fulltime Faculty." *Community College Review*, 1979, 6 (3), 65–72.

Gappa, J. M. *Parttime Faculty: Higher Education at the Crossroads*. Association for the Study of Higher Education Research Report No. 3, Clearinghouse on Higher Education, Washington, D.C., 1984.

Kellams, S. E., and Kyre, K. K. "Parttime Faculty in Four-Year Colleges and Universities." In D. W. Leslie (Ed.), *Employing Parttime Faculty*. New Directions for Institutional Research, no. 18. San Francisco: Jossey-Bass, 1978.

Leslie, D. (Ed.). *Employing Parttime Faculty*. San Francisco: Jossey-Bass, 1978.

Leslie, D., Kellams, S. and Gunne G. M. *Parttime Faculty in American Higher Education*. New York: Praeger, 1982.

Parsons, M. (Ed.). "Using Parttime Faculty Effectively." *New Directions for Community Colleges*, no. 30. San Francisco: Jossey-Bass, 1980.

Tuckman, H. P. "Parttime Faculty: Some Suggestions of Policy." *Change Magazine*, 1981, *13* (1), 8–10.

Judith L. McGaughey is dean of adult and continuing education at LaGuardia Community College of the City University of New York.

Maintaining faculty vitality in the face of heavy teaching loads and the unrelenting challenge of underprepared students requires conscious effort and planning on the part of faculty members and academic administrators.

Maintaining Faculty Vitality

Thelma C. Altshuler
Suzanne L. Richter

This report has been prepared by two community college professionals with a total of forty-two years of experience. The report therefore reflects the experiences of two people who might have experienced burnout a long time ago but who believe they have avoided it. In preparation of the report, several books and articles from professional journals have been consulted. Most of the report is, however, based on personal reflections, intuitions, and practical application of theory.

When asked, prior to the 1985 Super Bowl, about coaching burnout, Don Shula, coach of the Miami Dolphins, replied: "I don't know what it means. It wasn't around until a few years back, and now everybody is trying to protect against it. It's not in my vocabulary, and I don't want it to be. I won't even look in the dictionary" (Heller, 1984, p. 3).

Of course, Shula is a champion, a winner, and regarded as one of the best in his business. One wonders how different his statement would be if he had been fired several times, coached consistent cellar-dwellers, gone unrecognized at airports, and had almost no feelings of self-worth.

Although it is tempting to apply "burnout" to any number of disaffections with work, the term has a narrower definition. It is not exclusively boredom, depression, envy, fatigue, or a general desire to be doing something else. Pines, Aronson, and Karfy (1981) define the term as "the result of constant or repeated pressure associated with an intense involvement with people over long periods of time. Such intense involvement is particularly prevalent in health education and social service occupations, where professionals have a calling to take care of other people's psychological, social, and physical problems. Burnout is the painful realization that they can no longer help people in need" (p. 15). Physicians, dentists, social workers, and teachers are among those who experience burnout; it occurs to both the self-employed and to members of large bureaucratic structures, such as the community college.

Burnout suggests a lack of enthusiasm for facing another week of work, and it is in evidence, for instance, when faculty greet each other, ruefully recounting some new horror story about the conditions of work. Whether or not they feel it, they assume that burnout is common. How can they be expected to put up with another horde of graceless students, another barrage of memos from insensitive administrators? Nevertheless, although it seems to be a pervasive condition, it is not an unsolvable one.

The Reluctant Teacher

He never intended to teach. Still, while he waited for just the opportunity to make a name in his chosen field, teaching provided a reliable income. He put in his time, observed the rules, met classes — superficially performing the function of a faculty member. But his heart was somewhere else. The somewhere else may be equated to almost any field in the arts or any other field with more would-bes than can-bes. The painter whose work remains in the provinces reads with envy and mounting frustration about the acceptance in New York galleries of former colleagues. Meanwhile, she exists in what appears to her an alien environment — the community college. The few art studio classes she teaches contain ungifted students doing derivative work.

The reluctant teacher lives with a sense of personal failure, not doing what she wanted to do and sometimes taking out her frustration on the students. She may appear to be angry with them, storming at the students or even leaving class before the bell rings. "She says we're not prepared," says one student, "but we never know what she wants." To tell them more fully what she wants would be to admit that she has made a fulltime career of what had been intended to be a stopgap.

The Elitist Professor

Few of the faculty at a community college ever attended such an institution. As they regard the curriculum and even the architecture of the school that employs them, they may think fondly of the varied subject offerings and sprawling campuses of their memories. Have they stepped down? Surely in the old days everyone wrote better, studied harder, had a wider range of experience. The plight of the elitist is serious. In an ideal world, all students would arrive as well motivated as he remembers himself as a freshman. Attendance would be consistent, work turned in on time, assigned readings read, and so on.

If the elitist professor chooses to ignore the reality of his classes and remark, "This is after all a college," he can then make assignments requiring students to do things that he may mistakenly remember having done with ease at the age of eighteen. One such elitist has assigned a novel by Jane Austen to be read and analyzed by all students in a required English class. Students who complain of a lack of interest are reminded, "You're in college" as if reminding the student of his environment will be motivation enough. To assign a work less complex or closer to student interest would be to lower the standards of a beloved host of revered mentors.

For the elitist, even an unread reading list is a mark of pride, a document to be shown with pride to colleagues: "This is what my students are told to do," he remarks. Similarly, the required long research paper can be assigned without regard for the ability of the student to find a suitable topic, organize the material, or write the complete work without considerable assistance.

Burnout for the elitist is aggravated by reading student papers — their far too personal literary analyses, their errors in syntax, their misunderstandings of symbols and subtleties, and the whole list of student boners that entertain colleagues year after year.

When will it end? Never. There is no likelihood that the local high schools will suddenly graduate a crop of highly literate students eager to attend the two-year college. So the elitist faces more of the same, and despairs of his plight. What can he do? Opportunities to teach more gifted students may be unavailable. The salary, his roots in the community, and the unpaid mortgage hold him captive to a job he does not really like or understand. To replace him (if tenure rules allow) or to punish him by withholding perks is to lose valuable knowledge and experience.

Solutions for the fatigued elitist would be imaginative suggestions from colleagues he respects. The beloved Austen novel becomes gestions from colleagues he respects. The beloved Austen novel becomes an alternate assignment or one on a list. Writing assignments become more effective when they are shorter and written, at least partially, in class, where help is available for students who need it. The writing workshop, with its exercises by teachers recalling their own freshman years, can be a needed reminder of one's own youthful limitations. The elitist needs to compare current student work with his own actual student work from the same age. Friendly, informal sharing of successful classroom practices will often more readily be accepted from a colleague than from administrative fiat.

Repetition and Boredom

Still another cause of burnout is repetition of basic courses. A schedule for teaching five classes of elementary anything is tiresome to most faculty. Semester after semester, year after year, students arrive. For them everything seems fresh while for the faculty member everything seems old. Hamlet's words "How weary, stale, flat, and unprofitable" seem especially designed for the teacher of entry-level courses. The solution can be the opportunity to teach at least one course a year in an elective close to the faculty member's heart — even if the enrollment is below minimum standards. It is supportive of faculty morale to offer such courses on some basis: parttime or as an individual studies course. Such a course becomes a seminar, with faculty and students meeting to discuss and learn material that interests and excites them — an antidote to the drudgery of the required skills course.

Changing Subject Matter

Faculty are often teaching courses they never studied. The history professor probably never studied something called social studies. What he is teaching is probably an amalgam of history, sociology, and pop psychology with a little newspaper editorial thrown in. Aware that straight history (chronological and European) is unappealing to the current student population the history professor has probably served on a committee designing the new course considered more relevant to the clientele.

Even entry-level courses in one's own discipline might be tolerable. However, as the student population shifts, faculty are being called on to teach as a subject (whether granted credit for graduation or not) the skills once taken for granted by anyone in college. The skills subject may include reading, how to find an address, understand an advertisement, comment on the weather.

Faculty teaching a changed version of a once familiar course face a challenging task. It is not only difficult to teach students who require more frequent assignments, inducements to read in the form of "pop quizzes," detailed syllabi, and the passing back and forth of papers to be evaluated, but it is simply not what most of us were trained to do.

Signs of Burnout

Burnout manifests itself in physical and emotional exhaustion. An early sign is frequent, inexplicable absenteeism. Minor illness becomes the occasion for absences of over a week. Vacations extend into the first days of school. Frequent family emergencies require time off; substitutes may have to determine the final grades or stall students requiring personal attention.

Another sign is the dehumanizing of the client, as when the professional refers to clients in a derogatory way, as "junkies," "monsters," or the "great unwashed." For the community college teacher, one way to deal with his own disappointment is to stereotype the student as unworthy and to share, as humorously as possible, some of the student boners that are sure to appear.

For all but clockwatchers, cynics, and those counting the days until retirement, the hope remains that what has been said in class, assigned as homework, written on the board, and repeated has somehow been communicated. But the day the tests are collected brings evidence that, for at least some, no mental contact has been made. Assessing the tests means noting that one's own best personal efforts have not been understood. It is a rejection, not unlike explaining some deeply felt belief to a friend only to be asked, "But what do you mean? Why do you care about that stuff?" One response to this rejection is to share horror stories about students with other teachers. Release comes in repeated exchanges with colleagues.

Survival Tactics

Academic survival may well depend on these exchanges: "She even missed the same questions that I included from the last test"; and "She begged me for a make up exam and then didn't show up for two appointments"; and "This paper was supposed to be on the most memorable idea from the whole semester in this class, and here's a student who writes about falling in love with the kid in the next seat"; or "Even though my policy on absences is in capital letters on the course outline, this kid who's been absent half the time has the nerve to argue about his grade."

These faculty complaints are partly about students' failure to understand course content and partly outrage at their naiveté and lack of civility. Perhaps there are explanations for the complaints. A completely forbearing teacher might wonder if there is a language problem, or if years of habituation to other rules had made it hard for the student to recognize the greater responsibility of college.

At a more intense level than this ventilation and sharing is the totally negative approach of the faculty member so disappointed with his plight that he resists administrative programs and suggestions; in its most advanced state, this sort of negative response questions the validity of the college itself. Harnish and Creamer (1984) describe this behavior in a type they call "Charlie Critic": "He has a high energy level, is a creative individual, and has strong needs for challenge, diversity, and variety in his work. . . . Aware of the discrepancies between his expectations and the realities of the community college, and often seen as a troublemaker, misfit, or malcontent . . . he feels bored, trapped or 'stuck' in his present position" (p. 63).

The Charlie Critic type does not exhaust the possibilities of critics who move from their disappointment in students to the level of totally negative performance. It is possible that among the critics who take poor student performance as proof of their own superiority may be some who are responsible for that poor performance because of their own lack of creativity.

No solution may exist to the problem of the totally negative and basically uncreative teacher. Unwilling to change an assignment, unwilling to offer a wider choice of writing topics, unwilling even to change the format of a test that has previously confused even better students, this teacher injects cynicism into the goodnatured complaining of other faculty members.

The Course Syllabus

A current practice holds that objectives for students and faculty alike be spelled out. The course outline for students has become more and more specific, in some cases listing exactly what will occur on each day of the term. Clearly, such specificity may result in a feeling of speed that allows limited time for questions for students and no opportunity for variance from the outline. As students come to expect this rigidity, there is less opportunity for a more relaxed or natural pace or for digressions. This spelling out of expectations is useful, but it can be restrictive.

Making a detailed syllabus is arduous for many instructors. A syllabus for some courses runs to many pages. Faculty, perhaps with little preparation for the task, must list new terms; must point out the subheads that skilled readers would have automatically noticed; must guide the student through sample test questions; and must outline in detail exactly what amount and quality of work is expected for each grade, including penalties for absences, late arrivals to class, and failure to turn in work on time. Although these details are useful and expected, the need to specify what once was unnecessary has proved to be baffling, frustrating, and further cause for faculty disenchantment.

Help in designing these syllabi is useful, provided it allows curriculum control to remain in the hands of the faculty. Sample syllabi from other courses are useful as is sympathetic assistance.

Faculty Recognition

Similarly, faculty recognition is based on carefully enunciated objectives, with a quid pro quo for courses taken, degrees obtained, and service to the community. The goals set forth by management help to dispel suspicion about favoritism. But old timers may continue to believe that management by objectives contains too much of the corporate boardroom, and too little of academe as they believe it once was.

A Community of Strangers

There was a time, at least in some teachers' imaginations, when a small group of committed scholars gathered together to teach, meet with each other, and follow their pursuits with a minimum of interference by administrative superstructure.

The modern community college is clearly not such a place. Most faculty do not even know their colleagues. They do not live near each other, and they do not gather for tea or even an after-work beer.

Nevertheless, the image of self-directed faculty, meeting without regard for entrance scores, demographics, recruitment, and other intrusions by the administration is a persistent one. That that image is not true is the cause for disappointment.

Responses to Burnout

To be burned out is to despair over any prospects for gratifying teaching at the present school. What remains is a debilitating sense of lack of control, reflected in such statements as: "I'd rather be teaching in a four-year school," "I have no control over my decisions," "Nothing good will ever happen at this place," and "It doesn't matter what I do; the prizes go to others."

While the statements sound depressed, all depressed faculty are not victims of burnout. One may be temporarily disaffected or feel temporarily powerless. The true burnout victim, however, has an overwhelming sense of failure and loss of pride related to being in the wrong career at the wrong place for too long a time, with no prospects for change.

Successful cures for burnout involve self-knowledge and an administration sensitive to faculty frustration. Self-knowledge, that elusive goal, is no more widespread among community college faculty than in other segments of the population. It is, therefore, not surprising that some victims of burnout continue to stay in the very surroundings that cause them so much acute discomfort. The faculty member who claims, for instance, that he is better suited to a four-year college may be reluctant to face his own lack of scholarly qualifications for the desired change. With so many newly graduated Ph.D.s, the competition is formidable. If, when he accepted work at a two-year school, there had been the option of a university appointment, would he have developed the energy and discipline to do research and to publish? Or would he just have burned out at a different institution?

Those who know themselves sometimes would admit, "I'd rather be teaching well-prepared students... but without the additional responsibilities of research."

Some perpetually disgruntled teachers should decide for themselves to quit teaching. Once they are in a new field, they may well wonder how they endured their old life for so long.

Others need to retrain in a teaching discipline that is more attractive. One department head, after years of futile attempts to improve teaching and the quality of students in an arts program, has found new energy after retraining in computers. Her old job resulted in the powerlessness that is a key ingredient of burnout. Nothing—not the publication of manifestos, review of syllabi, or years of meetings for curriculum change or staff development—had resulted in the department she had envisioned. Finally, she had the good sense to recognize that some jobs could be left to others. She is now teaching in the same institution, but doing what she enjoys doing.

Institutional Responsibilities

A viable institution assumes some responsibility for the well-being of its employees, be it physical or mental. Plans must be made to avoid what can be potentially damaging and to keep faculty vital and creative. At Miami-Dade Community College, the administration and faculty have developed such plans. They do not always work, but some examples demonstrate institutional commitment to psychological well-being.

For example, Miami-Dade has always endeavored to hire faculty for a full year. Because enrollment was less in the summers, the work load was a combination of teaching and projects, many of which were insignificant. Looking at a three-year period, Robert H. McCabe, president of Miami-Dade, proposed that all faculty have summers off with pay, two of every three summers. The same number of courses are still taught over the three-year period but more rest and recreation is built in.

As another example, Miami-Dade reconfigured its traditional sabbaticals so that faculty who were willing and able could take courses to retrain for teaching in other disciplines. Campuses have the option to award a certain number of released classes per semester to a social science teacher with an undergraduate minor in math as support for her acquiring skills and graduate credits in mathematics. With the emphasis on information skills, such retraining is necessary for both the individual and the institution.

Although Miami-Dade does not have what is defined as merit pay, salary scales in each academic rank have been adjusted so that promotion brings with it more than just recognition. For administrators and support personnel, bonuses are available each year as reward for excellent performance.

If an institution does not systematically provide options designed to negate boredom, encourage creativity, and reward performance, then the institution will be doomed to burnout. If, however, an institution demonstrates such commitment, individual administrators have leeway to support faculty on a more personal level.

The Administrator

An administrator's job is to be alert to burnout signs and provide preventive medicine. Once burnout occurs, as with other traumatic illnesses, the case may be terminal. Roueche (1985) reported that the study on excellence in the community college recently completed at the University of Texas confirmed previous studies that found that the primary reward for outstanding teachers is the intrinsic one that comes from students who respond, learn, and progress. The problem, of course, is distinguishing between the teacher who can spend five years teaching beginning piano and still approach each student as an individual and the teacher who after five years is no longer certain how the scales should sound.

The Curriculum

One of the easiest ways to avoid burnout resulting from repetition is to avoid a static curriculum, an accomplished fact at many community colleges. English teachers, for example, should be encouraged to select new readings every three years. Learning resources centers should consciously order replacement films for those films that are shown over and over. This would also induce the teacher to stay in the classroom and demonstrate interest, not boredom, to the students.

Curriculum cycles seem never ending. Presently, deciding which is more important — the computer or writing across the curriculum — is itself not as significant as is administrative encouragement to learn something new — some intriguing resource or varied technique. An administrator can always begin a pilot program or hire a consultant. One does not have to revise the curriculum totally to keep it vital; one just has to be alert to trends and guarantee that all the faculty are exposed to some of what is new: offer workshops and graduate computer courses, develop computing throughout the curriculum, and reward faculty accordingly.

Variety

Strategies, too, can be constructive in aiding the teacher to receive their intrinsic rewards. If one lectures to large groups, perhaps that special response from the individual student is hidden among the numbers. The instructor should work on structuring the curriculum with small discussion groups to support lecture sections and encourage keeping a written journal. As one learns more about the process, the process becomes more important; the distance between teacher and learner narrows and communication becomes more direct. Some variety in the classes each faculty teaches is necessary, even if it is only variety in the time of day of classes. Teaching evening classes may relieve some tedium because of more student diversity in the classroom. Faculty should be encouraged to participate in continuing education teaching experiences.

This year at our campus we at Miami-Dade have opened our

doors to a junior high gifted program that offers extra money and some different challenges to interested faculty. All of our campuses have summer programs for the gifted and talented. Again, there may be administrative headaches, but these provide intellectual change and challenge.

Appreciation

As in other professions, lack of appreciation is a major cause of burnout. Perhaps the faculty member is in an anomalous position because there is no direct supervision of what is said and done in the classroom. Thus, recognition appears most often as the result of outside activities — service on committees, ability to attract favorable public attention for speakers, and other extra functions. Recognition of an outstanding job may be equated with hours spent on campus or with close adherence to posted office hours.

The community college supposedly emphasizes teaching and rewards outstanding teaching. Student evaluations should be encouraged. While many may view such evaluations as naive at best and pejorative at worst, such evaluations can provide valuable information to the teacher. The classroom teachers need to know how they are perceived and valued. After all, we entered this profession not to make money or become famous but to contribute to helping others make this a much better world. We need our students to tell us how well we are doing our jobs.

Sharing

Encourage classroom visitations by chairpersons and peers. If a visit of a tenured full professor by a much younger and less experienced teacher seems superfluous, consider the potential for dialogue, for sharing, for mentoring. For the most part, evaluations are positive. Although not designed to make people feel good, they generally do because of the quality of teachers. Whatever forms invite consensus (climate surveys, student evaluations, classroom visits, peer evaluation) should be used to support and nurture a sense of professionalism.

Administrative Consistency

An administrator should be consistent. If one writes a congratulatory memo for a job poorly done as well as for one well done, then the memos are worthless. If the outstanding teacher is promoted right alongside the person who figuratively retired three years ago, then the promotion is an insult. Administrators should make it clear what is of value and stress that. They should utilize prerogatives — special committee assignments, travel, invitations — to reward good performance.

Emphasize Teaching

As the promotion of teaching excellence becomes a priority, more people besides teachers will value it. Much of the burnout in our profession comes from people who are in the wrong profession, but some of us who like our profession get tired of the heavy workload and the low salary. We need to emphasize what teaching means; we need to involve the community and alumni and we need to develop more teaching excellence.

Summary

Perhaps burnout in the community college is the equivalent of midlife crisis in our personal lives. The community college movement has come of age; no longer fresh and new, it must struggle with the same problems we as individuals do — identity, aging, and change.

An administrator, if he or she has not been able to prevent burnout, needs to respond to burnout cases immediately. Often a good person can be in the wrong job at the college. The administrator should know the faculty and their strengths. There should be a referral system for those who may need to talk through issues. Quick, humanistic action is vital because one person crying "Burnout" is like the cry of "fire" in the theatre — the cry spreads as quickly as the fire. The disease, although preventible, certainly is contagious.

The solution is to be alert; to design our systems to include people support, and to understand the potential for problems, such as burnout, in a profession such as ours. But the solution, like so many, is complex. "Know thyself" helps but only if the administration responds and hears the real cries for help.

References

Harnish, D., and Creamer, D. G. "Understanding and Combating Community College Faculty Professional Stagnation." *The Journal of Staff, Program, and Organization Development,* 1984, *2* (3), 62–67.
Heller, D. "People in Sports," *Miami Herald,* December 22, 1984, Section 7, p. 3.

Pines, A. M., Aronson, E., and Karfy, D. *Burnout: From Tedium to Personal Growth.* New York: Macmillan Free Press, 1981.

Roueche, J. "Access with Quality: A Study of Teaching Excellence in American Community Colleges." Remarks in a workshop at the Annual Convention of the American Association of Community and Junior Colleges, San Diego, California, April 15, 1985.

Thelma C. Altshuler is professor of humanities at Miami-Dade Community College.

Suzanne L. Richter is dean of instruction, Wolfson Campus, Miami-Dade Community College.

Increasing state control, which is adding to the complexity of community college governance, requires new skills of community college leaders.

Maintaining Integrity in a State System

Donald E. Puyear

One of the major challenges facing a community college leader is ensuring that the comprehensive services and programs required by the mission of the college are available, are of high quality, are adequately staffed and funded, and are understood by the citizens of the service region. The governance process that makes this task possible became increasingly complicated with the rise of state systems of community colleges and other state level coordinating bodies.

The governance of community college is handled differently in each state. These differences are great and span the philosophical spectrum from substantial local autonomy to very close state control. Any generalization about dealing with state level coordinating or governing bodies must, therefore, be examined for applicability and then carefully adapted to any specific situation. Nonetheless, the pervasiveness of state coordination and control and the effect that it can have on the operation, development, and philosophy of a community college makes it an issue of considerable importance.

While it is tempting to equate institutional integrity with local autonomy, this simplistic equation often is not sufficient. If institutional integrity is considered to be the degree to which the institution is able to remain true to its basic mission, state level coordination can either enhance or threaten the integrity of the community colleges within a state. Much depends upon the nature of the governance structure of the state and its relationship to the campus.

Variety of State Organizations

The Alaska State Commission on Postsecondary Education (1981) examined the postsecondary educational structures of the fifty states and described their organization in terms of the following six classifications (pp. 108–109):
1. Community college governance or coordination exists separate from other public higher education (thirty states).
2. Community colleges are under an all encompassing educational agency — kindergarten through post-secondary (two states).
3. Community colleges are under an all encompassing coordinating or governing agency for postsecondary education only (six states).
4. Community college governance or coordination is divided between two or more agencies (seven states).
5. Community colleges are exclusively part of the university (four states).
6. No community colleges (one state).

While useful, these classifications still mask important differences in the governance responsibilities of state level bodies. The point is that each state has developed a different mechanism for governing community colleges. The state's history, the method of establishing and funding community colleges, the constitutional or statutory authority of local college boards and the state level board, the taxing and borrowing authority of the colleges, the relationship among the community colleges and between community colleges and other publicly supported educational institutions, and many other important variables differ among the states.

It would be inappropriate and of little value to attempt to critique the relative advantages or disadvantages of the various state systems. Existing systems must be dealt with as they are. Community college leaders in each state must thoroughly understand the governance structure of that state and, to the extent possible, understand how that particular structure evolved and how it is evolving. With this knowledge they will be better equipped to protect institutional integrity in the system and, should it become appropriate, to propose needed improvements.

State Control Is Increasing

State control is increasing at the expense of local autonomy. The literature provides ample documentation of this trend. There is less agreement on why this may be so; different authors cite various reasons, all of which probably contribute to the overall effect. State legislatures, executive agencies, and coordinating bodies are becoming increasingly involved in college budgeting, personnel administration, program management, and planning (Zoglin, 1977; Darnowski, 1978; Campbell, 1978; Stalcup and others, 1978). A number of federal programs mandate state agencies or commissions to receive and monitor federal funds flowing to educational institutions (Bender, 1975; Kintzer, 1980). "Government in the Sunshine" and other laws directed at issues outside of higher education have been shown to affect community college functions and have also taken their toll on institutional autonomy (Martorana and Smutz, 1980; Martorana and Broomal, 1981, 1982; Martorana and Corbett, 1983; Martorana and Garland, 1984; Martorana and others, 1985).

The increasing cost of all social programs and the budget squeeze brought on by the recessionary period of the early 1980s have made state legislators more sensitive to the costs of community colleges. The leveling of community college enrollments as the baby boom generation passes beyond the years of highest college attendance has made it appear that community college costs should also stabilize. Legislators are inclined to intervene when this stabilization does not occur with the result of greater state control.

The increase in state control may be inevitable. There should be a law of political reality that states: The highest governmental level that contributes financially to the operation of an enterprise will eventually exercise disproportionate control over that enterprise. Corollaries to this law might include: This control will increase in times of scarce resources but will, at best, stabilize in times of greater affluence. Also, if information is available that appears to provide a basis for control or evaluation, it will be used for those purposes.

The ingredients for increased state control are present—community colleges cannot do without state funds, times of scarce resources are recent enough to be on the minds of state legislators, and the omnipresent computer is making the centralization and aggregation of data routine.

There is no agreement as to whether state coordination is, in itself, bad. Bender (1975) urges community college leaders to try to reverse the trend. He goes so far as to state:

> Community-based community colleges cannot be viewed as state-owned or operated institutions. Too frequently, state legislatures view them as a state agency rather than a state government corporation receiving a state subsidy for their operation (which is) the appropriate model....(p. 55).

Darnowski (1978) argues that, in Connecticut, the maze of state agencies imposing checks on college fiscal and personnel management now results in

> ...a feeling on the part of college administrators that their power to make decisions is meaningless in the face of overwhelming power of various agencies to contradict them. It would not be unreasonable to expect normal people to react by *not* making decisions... resigning themselves to whatever results occurs "up in Hartford" (p. 15).

Stalcup and others (1978) assert even more strongly that:

> The hard truth is that local control and state level coordination are partners in a marriage that was preordained to fail in spite of the rhetoric of the community/junior college historians.... State and federal legislation, guidelines, and regulations effectively preclude unilateral actions by institutions except in pedestrian matters (p. 34).

On the other hand, Miner (1979) states a position that must also be considered:

> Very often external intervention is a statement of real and viable public opinion about the perceived value of education or a statement about the direction education should be taking (p. 2).

Mundt (1978) takes this even further:

> There is still another dimension. We are tax-supported institutions.... People as a whole, and thus their elected representatives, want to know what it is that their dollars are purchasing.... Above all, there is little point in decrying the demise of local control or the rise of state control, for neither is a correct description of what is happening. Rather, higher education decision making... is now based on a complex interactive process involving many interests, and will probably continue that way for some time to come (p. 60).

Kintzer (1980) summarizes the situation effectively when he states:

> The proliferation of state systems and the continuing shift toward state government control are again the most crucial organizational developments of the decade. This direction need not be considered entirely unfortunate. A certain level of coordination is necessary. The search for balance appropriate for individual

states will continue to test the ingenuity of politicians and educators alike (p. 30).

Attempts to turn the tide of increasing state coordination and control are probably futile. Striving to ensure that the state coordination or control is focused on appropriate issues and capitalizing on the potential advantages of greater coordination may be more productive strategies for community college leaders to pursue. Martorana and Smutz (1980) urge community college leaders to develop political skills. They go so far as to state:

> Politics and postsecondary education were never completely separate, but they are more intimately related now than in the past. How community college leaders perform in the political arena will have a substantial impact on how the issues of the appropriate realms of responsibility and local control are ultimately decided (pp. 12–13).

The Nature of State Control

There are at least three major facets of state control that impact on the governance of community colleges. They are: (1) legislative intervention, (2) oversight or involvement by central state agencies dealing with operational matters, and (3) state level coordinating or governing boards with their related administrative staff. While all of these can affect the operation of community colleges, they are very different phenomena.

Legislative Intervention. For most of the past decade Martorana and his colleagues at the Center for the Study of Higher Education, The Pennsylvania State University, have been reviewing legislation affecting community colleges. Several important trends appear from this work:

Increasing Volume of Legislation. Martorana and Garland (1984, p. 6) report an almost ten-fold increase in reported legislation affecting community colleges since the studies began in 1976. Note, however, that at least some of the apparent increase is likely due to more thorough reporting. Martorana's work has created heightened interest in this topic.

Community Colleges often Are not the Primary Focus. Most of the legislation affecting community colleges was not drafted with them as the major focus. The largest category of reported legislation has consistently been intended for all of postsecondary education, which has been just under half of the total throughout these studies, and legislation intended for state bodies in general, which has been about one third of the total. The share of legislation specifically directed toward community colleges has decreased from just over 30 percent in 1978 and 1979 to just over 20 percent in 1981 and 1982. (Martorana and Broomal, 1982, p. 78; Martorana and Corbett, 1983, p. 62; Martorana and others, 1985, p. 4).

Most Concern is for Nonacademic Matters. Finance, administration, and personnel issues consistently dominate the lists of legislative proposals, rising to 78 percent of the total in 1982 (Martorana and Corbett, 1983, p. 77). However, in a recent report, Martorana and others (1985, p. 4) stated that tuition issues, including classification of students for tuition purposes and the extension of tuition benefits to special groups, continue to receive considerable attention. The number of bills regarding academic programs declined from 12.2 percent of the total in 1978 to 4.7 percent in 1982 (Martorana and Corbett, 1983, p. 77); however, Martorana and Garland (1984, p. 7) reported a remarkable 227 percent increase in activity for this category in 1983, primarily in the area of special programs concerned with job training and retraining. This heightened level of activity was not, however, continued into 1984 (Martorana and others, 1985, p. 4).

Legislation only incidentally directed toward community colleges (concerned with freedom of information, conflict of interest, procurement requirements, employment practices, budget and fiscal management, and other similar matters) has had a profound effect on the operation of community colleges in many states. In Virginia, for example, a recent change in the state's freedom of information statute prohibited the use of conference calls to conduct business. The result has been to require additional meetings of the State Board for Community Colleges—with some members traveling great distances—to approve minor, but urgent construction bids and easements. Also, financial disclosure statements required under Virginia's conflict of interest statute have caused some well qualified business persons to decline appointment to local college advisory boards. While many such statutes are intended to, and do, curtail abuse of power and enhance accountability in government, they also cause community college procedures to become less responsive to the college's needs—the procedures tend to become increasingly formal and have relatively more emphasis on process than results.

Central State Agencies. Another form of incidental control comes from central state agencies that are charged with some aspect of the operation of government such as budget management, personnel, accounting, facilities, procurement, data processing, and the like. As Darnowski (1978) noted, dealing with such agencies can be extremely difficult. The central agency's concern is that the particular function for which it has responsibility is conducted in accordance with applicable laws and regulations. It has no responsibility for the college accomplishing its mission and, since central state agencies are usually remote from the college's service region, it is insulated from any negative reactions to its activities. The problem is not that the people in the central state agencies are bad—often they are very skilled in their tasks and, as individuals, sympathetic to the needs of the college—but rather that each agency's portion of the overall operation is dealt with in absolute terms by that agency. The nature of the system is such that they cannot make the reasoned compromises between competing requirements that are needed for optimum operation of a complex organization such as a comprehensive community college.

While central state agencies, operating as described above, assure a relatively high level of compliance with regulations and tend to prevent state officials from taking inappropriate advantage of their positions, they clearly stifle initiative. Indeed, stifling inappropriate initiative is among the purposes of such agencies.

Many community college activities relate to more than one central state agency. When several agencies have to review and approve an action, delay is certain. It is nearly impossible for a new, creative proposal to survive when it must be reviewed, in sequence, by several central state agencies. The safe approach, practiced by survivors in central agencies, mandates that if it is not already standard practice it is suspect; if it is suspect some reason should be found to reject or modify it. The resulting paralysis is dangerous to the health of community colleges.

It is difficult, but perhaps not impossible, to reverse the flow of control to central state agencies. In Virginia, for example, the presidents of the state's colleges and universities (including community colleges) took the initiative to describe some needed modifications in state procedures. Members of the governor's cabinet convened a high level task force on decentralization that meets regularly. While it is far too early to report specific accomplishments, there is reason to believe that at least some meaningful improvements will result.

Governing and Coordinating Boards. When the issue of state control arises, first consideration is usually given to the formal structure the state has developed for the governance of community colleges. This is as it should be, for the governance structure affects community college integrity in many ways. As was previously stated, there is considerable variety in state level governance structures and a community college leader must learn to deal effectively with the structure that exists in his or her state. Further, as has also been discussed above, much of the state's involvement with community college operation comes from outside the formal higher education governance structure. Nonetheless, higher education governing and coordinating boards have a special obligation to ensure that individual community colleges (and any other education institutions that may be involved) have sufficient flexibility and authority to maintain institutional integrity. Unlike legislative bodies and central state agencies, higher education boards have staffs that should thoroughly understand the missions of the institutions for which they have responsibility. Properly led and properly staffed state level boards can be instrumental in preserving institutional integrity.

The importance of leadership was underscored by Bender (1975) when he stated:

> Success or failure of state level boards or agencies normally is dependent more on the role of the personalities than on the structure or range of powers of the organization (p. 35).

This observation helps to explain why some systems seem to work so much better than others despite apparent similarities in their structure. A well led, sensitive, state level board or agency can enhance institutional effectiveness in a number of ways, the more important of which include the following items.

Advocacy. Interpreting the community college mission to legislative bodies, executive agencies, and to the public at large can often be done more effectively by a respected state level advocate than by representatives of the various colleges alone. By jointly developing a specific plan of legislative priorities, and sticking with the plan, community colleges can improve their legislative effectiveness. Bender (1975) relates:

> State level advocacy for community colleges is needed.... While some administrators and faculty would argue such a function could be achieved outside the governmental structure through a voluntary organization, such is not true. Statewide public good must take precedence over institutional self-interest (p. 55).

Accountability. By providing community colleges with a vehicle for demonstrating their accountability to their mission, the state level board or agency can improve the college's image and reduce the probability that other agencies will attempt to impose accountability to less appropriate criteria. Program and service region coordination and approval helps to demonstrate that resources are being used effectively and the inappropriate duplication is minimized.

Running Interference. The apparent single-minded rule enforcing inflexibility of central state agencies represents one of the more debilitating aspects of state involvement in the operation of a comprehensive community college. Since the state level board or agency and central state agencies are usually located in the capital city, personnel from the two agencies can get to know each other and often can develop a useful dialogue that assists central state agency personnel in understanding the problems and needs of the colleges, and vice versa. This can serve to reduce misunderstandings and assist communication.

Equitable Resources. By distributing resources in a consistent, rational manner, the state level board or agency can assure that all community colleges are provided equitable resources. This, of course, would not be considered to be an advantage by a college that feels it could do better on its own. However, if the "rich get richer and the poor get poorer" then community college education in general will suffer.

Accessibility. If the state level board or agency has the responsibility for locating community colleges and defining their service regions, it is more likely that all of the citizens of the state will receive community college educational opportunities. If the location of community colleges is left entirely to local initiative, poorer regions of the state may not have them. Citizens of these areas (who probably also have poorer public schools) will, through their state taxes, be contributing to the support of community colleges in the more affluent areas without receiving corresponding benefits.

The likelihood that the state level agency will be sensitive and effective will be enhanced, Angel (1982) suggests, by the following actions. He speaks from the college perspective:

Attitude Adjustment. [We resent any intrusion in college activities, but] it is high time that we accept what we already know—that the autonomy of institutions of higher education neither can be nor should be complete. The public has a fair interest in their conduct (p. 8).

Quality Staffing. It is tempting to conclude that higher education would be better off [if the state level agency had] less staff or staff who have little interest or expertise in the postsecondary world .... Tempting, but foolish! Adequate staff who understand and have some solid academic credentials will be a major part of improving the future (p. 9).

Information Needs. We live in an information age, and management at all levels must have timely, accurate, and comprehensive hard data upon which to base its difficult and strategic decisions (p. 9).

Communications. Public support of higher education . . . has dissipated. [The colleges and the state level agency] are going to have to work together if we are going to revitalize higher education (p. 10).

Institutional Integrity Defined

As indicated in the opening paragraphs of this chapter, one should not confuse the concepts of institutional autonomy and institutional integrity. Autonomy describes a situation in which the institution can determine its own course without outside interference; integrity connotes that the institution's actions are consistent with an established code of values. The mission of the college is, of course, that code of values. Thus, institutional integrity is present only when an institution has a clearly defined mission and consistently acts in accordance with the requirements and limitations of that mission.

Clearly, an autonomous institution can have institutional integrity, or not. An autonomous institution can and does compromise its integrity in pursuit of short-term gains. When a college dilutes the quality of a program to satisfy enrollment goals, despite the fact that the quality of its programs will ultimately define the college's value to the community, or when it creates an inappropriate program simply to get a grant, it has lost integrity.

On the other hand, to the degree that a college lacks autonomy, it lacks the assurance that it can adhere to its mission. One must distinguish here between the legitimate right of a state legislature to define the basic mission of that state's community colleges and the inappropriate (and often inconsistent) intrusions into the operation of the colleges. These latter intrusions are often little more than reactions to some perceived abuse or lack of responsiveness on the part of one or two colleges and they do compromise institutional integrity.

The Need for a Better Definition of Mission

The first prerequisite for institutional integrity is a clear sense of the mission of the college. In the first two chapters of this volume, both Wagoner and Vaughan demonstrate that community colleges are still seeking a consistent statement of mission that is understood by educators, legislators, and the populace alike. Unfortunately, the scope of the community college mission, as expounded by some community college leaders, has regularly expanded until the accusation that community colleges desire to be "all things to all people" has become reasonably justified. Vaughan (1983) argues forcefully for a more articulate statement of mission when he states that

> ... literally hundreds of times each year community college presidents tell local service clubs and various other audiences that the community college "is unique," "is uniquely American," "cares about students," "serves the total community," and that its faculty members are "employed to teach and not research." These, and any number of similar statements, shed little light on the mission of the community college.... Legislators certainly deserve (and are demanding) more than warmed-over phrases when they are asked to appropriate the millions of dollars requested by community colleges (p. 11).

Statements of mission that set few limits and shun the establishment of priorities do little to create a sense of confidence on the part of legislators that community college leaders understand what they are doing or that they will make what the legislators consider to be appropriate use of the funds that are appropriated. In the absence of a clear sense of mission shared by community college leaders and legislators, can it be a surprise that legislators sometimes act as though community colleges need guidance in how appropriated funds are to be used?

If institutional integrity is to be maintained, a new consensus regarding the mission of comprehensive community colleges must be developed. The resulting statement of mission must be more precise than most statements that have been in vogue in the past. Vaughan's suggestions in the second chapter of this volume may provide an appropriate beginning for developing such a statement.

While a national consensus on the mission of the comprehensive community college is desirable, it is even more important that the community colleges in a state have a high level of consistency as they interpret their mission to the legislature and other constituencies. The central state coordinating agency can and should play a central role in bringing about such consistency.

Summary

State involvement in the operation of community colleges is increasing and is likely to continue to increase in the foreseeable future. Increased state control makes the job of community college leaders more difficult and can cause colleges to become less responsive to the needs of their communities. State level coordination, however, also has its positive side. There is likely to be greater accountability, better planning, fairer allocation of resources, and more general access to community colleges when a sensitive coordinating agency is involved.

Further, a sensitive state level coordinating agency can be helpful in developing and articulating a statement of mission that can be understood by legislators and others outside of the educational fraternity. Such a mission statement is the first prerequisite of institutional integrity.

References

Alaska State Commission on Postsecondary Education. *Community Colleges: A Report to the Twelfth Alaska State Legislature by the Community College Interim Committee.* (Vol. 1.) Juneau: Alaska State Commission on Postsecondary Education, 1981.

Angel, D. "Nailing Jello to the Wall. Forum: What Progress Are the States Making in Initiating Higher Education Reform?" Paper presented to the Annual Meeting of the American Council on Education, Minneapolis, Minn., October 1982.

Bender, L. W. *The State, Communities, and Control of the Community College: Issues and Recommendations.* Washington, D.C.: American Association of Community and Junior Colleges, 1975.

Campbell, R. "Local Control—Myth or Reality." *Community and Junior College Journal.* 1978, *48*(8), 48–50.

Darnowski, V. S. "The Maze in Connecticut." In S. F. Charles (Ed.), *Balancing State and Local Control.* New Directions for Community Colleges, no. 23. San Francisco: Jossey-Bass, 1978.

Kintzer, F. C. *Organization and Leadership of Two-Year Colleges: Preparing for the Eighties.* Institute of Higher Education Topical Paper. Gainesville: Institute of Higher Education, University of Florida, 1980.

Martorana, S. V., and Broomal, J. K. *State Legislation Affecting Community and Junior Colleges, 1980.* Report no. 37. University Park: Center for the Study of Higher Education, Pennsylvania State University, 1981.

Martorana, S. V., and Broomal, J. K. *State Legislation Affecting Community, Junior, and Two-Year Technical Colleges, 1981.* Report no. 38. University Park: Center for the Study of Higher Education, Pennsylvania State University and the National Council of State Directors of Community-Junior Colleges, 1982.

Martorana, S. V., and Corbett, P. C. *State Legislation Affecting Community, Junior, and Two-Year Technical Colleges, 1982.* Report no. 39. University Park: Center for the Study of Higher Education, Pennsylvania State University and the National Council of State Directors of Community-Junior Colleges, 1983.

Martorana, S. V., and Garland, P. H. "Highlights and Overview of Actions in 1983 State Legislative Sessions Affecting Community and Two-Year Technical Colleges: A Report to the National Council of State Directors of Community-Junior Colleges." University Park: Center for the Study of Higher Education, The Pennsylvania State University, 1984.

Martorana, S. V., Garland, P. H., and Blake, P. D. "State Legislation Affecting Community, Junior, and Two-Year Technical Colleges, 1984: A Preliminary Report to the National Council of State Directors of Community-Junior Colleges (NCSDCJC)." University Park: Center for the Study of Higher Education, The Pennsylvania State University, 1985.

Martorana, S. V., and Smutz, W. D. "State Legislation, Politics, and Community Colleges." *Community College Review*, 1980 *7*(3), 5–13.

Miner, N. "External Intervention: Past, Present, and Future." Unpublished paper, Seminole Community College, Sanford, Florida, 1979.

Mundt, J. C. "State versus Local Control: Reality and Myth Over Concern for Local Autonomy." In S. F. Charles (Ed.), *Balancing State and Local Control*. New Directions for Community Colleges, no. 23. San Francisco: Jossey-Bass, 1978.

Stalcup, R., Lester, P., and Wilson, J. "Local Control of Community Colleges: Myth and Reality." *Community College Frontiers*, 1978, 6(2), 33-36.

Vaughan, G. B. "Introduction: Community Colleges in Perspective." In G. B. Vaughan and Associates, *Issues for Community College Leaders in a New Era*. San Francisco: Jossey-Bass, 1983.

Zoglin, M. L. *Understanding and Influencing the State Role in Postsecondary Education*. Management Report 77/7. Cupertino: Association of California Community College Administrators, 1977.

Donald E. Puyear is deputy chancellor of the Virginia Community College System. Prior to assuming his current position, in 1983, he was president of Central Virginia Community College.

Material abstracted from recent additions to the Educational Resources Information Center (ERIC) system provides further information on issues related to institutional integrity.

Sources and Information: Maintaining Institutional Integrity

Jim Palmer
Diane Zwemer

This concluding chapter provides an annotated bibliography of ERIC documents and journal articles dealing with major issues that impinge upon the institutional integrity of community colleges. The items cited in this bibliography were selected from ERIC's *Resources in Education* and *Current Index to Journals in Education* and cover the time period from January 1983 through July 1985. The bibliography is divided into five sections that list items on: (1) assessing the mission of the community college, (2) assessing the quality of community college education, (3) maintaining an effective faculty, (4) the effects and management of retrenchment, and (5) the state role in community college education.

Those items marked with an "ED" number are ERIC documents and can be obtained on microfiche at over 650 libraries across the country or ordered at the cost of reproduction and mailing from the ERIC Document Reproduction Service (EDRS) in Alexandria, Virginia. For an EDRS order form and a list of the libraries in your state that have ERIC microfiche collections, please contact the ERIC Clearinghouse for Junior Colleges, 8118 Math-Science Building, UCLA, 405 Hilgard, Los Angeles, California 90024.

Assessing the Mission of the Community College

Institutional integrity is tied to the college's mission and to the extent to which there is public understanding of and consensus with the role played by community colleges within the American higher education system. The documents and journal articles listed in this section of the bibliography focus on the struggle of community college practitioners to define the institutional mission of two-year colleges. Included in these documents are:
1. Documents which defend, criticize, or otherwise comment on the comprehensive, all-encompassing function of the community college curriculum (Alfred, 1984; Cohen, 1983; Cosand, 1983; Koltai, 1984; Minnesota State Community College Board, 1984; Townsend, 1984; Williams and Atwell, 1984).
2. Surveys that have been conducted to assess differences in the opinions of administrators, faculty, students, and the public concerning the proper role of the community college (Armenta and Richardson, 1984; Harrison and Rajasekhara, 1984; Highum, 1984; Richardson and Doucette, 1984; and Smith and others, 1982).
3. Examinations of the role of community colleges in increasing educational access through the open door (Boss, 1982; Hyde, 1982; National Council of State Directors of Community-Junior Colleges, 1983; Richardson, 1983; and Wattenbarger, 1983).
4. Discussions of the role played by community colleges in vocational education and economic development (American Association of Community and Junior Colleges, 1984; Long, 1984; McMullen, 1984; Parsons, 1983; Tyree and McConnell, 1982; and Vogler, 1984).

Alfred, R. L. "Paradox for Community College Education in the 80s." *Community College Review*, 1984, *12* (1), 2–6.

Argues that the community college's identity in higher education can no longer rest solely on low cost, open access, and comprehensiveness. Notes that other institutions, including nonunionized four-year colleges and proprietary schools, can now perform these same roles and that the community college needs a "new conceptualization of uniqueness." Calls on college leaders to formulate new roles rather than try to perpetuate the old.

American Association of Community and Junior Colleges. *Putting America Back to Work: The Kellogg Leadership Initiative. A Report and Guidebook.* Washington, D.C.: The Association, 1984. 66 pp. (ED 245 738).

Examines the economic climate of the United States and the role of the community college in economic recovery. Includes an outline of the origins and initial activities of the Putting America Back to Work Project, which was founded by the Kellogg Foundation to identify ways community colleges could contribute to economic recovery and introduce college resources to the leaders of private business and industry. Also presents an extensive list of possible activities that community colleges can pursue in economic and human resource development.

Armenta, R. R., and Richardson, R. C., Jr. "Opinions of Strategic Constituencies Regarding Community College Activities at Maricopa and Central Arizona College." Unpublished paper, [1984]. 8 pp. (ED 250 038).

Details the findings of a study conducted to compare the priorities of college administrators with those of strategic external constituencies regarding the activities of the Maricopa Community Colleges and Central Arizona College. Describes the study methodology, which involved a survey of various college constituents who were asked if each of sixty activities was "important to do" and whether it should be "funded with tax dollars." Compares responses of administrators with the responses of state board members, state legislators, and a sample of registered voters.

Boss, R. S. "Junior College Articulation: Admission, Retention, Transfer. A Position Paper." Graduate seminar paper, University of Maryland at College Park, 1982. 17 pp. (ED 231 484).

Notes the objections of many community college critics who posit that open access leads to an influx of ill-prepared students and erodes institutional quality. Maintains, however, that transfer to the university is not the sole measure of community college quality in that the colleges provide alternative avenues to success. Concludes that "the 'cooling-out' function in the junior college often works to make a mediocre scholar into a first-rate artist or competent craftsman" (p. 13).

Cohen, A. M. "Understanding the Transfer Function in California." *Community College Review*, 1983, *10* (4), 18–23.

Traces factors that have contributed to the erosion of the transfer function in California. Argues that college freshmen in California have always had the option of entering a four-year institution (if qualified) and that the community colleges have thus developed as adjunctive institutions that never played a clearly defined role in the educational pipeline to the baccalaureate. Calls for efforts to strengthen the transfer function, maintaining the "transfer function must not be allowed to slip out of the community college by inadvertence or because college spokespersons think they must promote different missions" (p. 22).

Cosand, J. "Who Will Make the Decisions?" *Community College Review*, 1983, *10* (4), 24–29.

Maintains that the comprehensive, open-door philosophy of the community college, as well as its commitment to serving local needs, is misunderstood by many persons who are in a position to affect the future of community colleges. Lists ten missions of the community college and argues that "institutional decision makers must . . . be prepared through commitment and aggressive action to educate and exert pressure on the state and federal decision makers . . . who are still ignorant or emotionally opposed to the philosophy of the comprehensive community colleges" (p. 27).

Harrison, W. L., and Rajasekhara, K. *Dundalk Community College Goals Survey Report*. Baltimore, Md.: Dundalk Community College, 1984. 49 pp. (ED 243 525).

Summarizes findings of a study conducted at Dundalk Community College to identify and prioritize basic college goals. Notes study methodology, which involved the use of a modified version of the Community College Goals Inventory. Details findings by respondent group: administrators, full-time and part-time faculty, full-time and part-time students, community citizens, and representatives of business and industry. Argues that reduced college funding requires administrators to use such surveys in prioritizing college missions and determining what activities will be funded.

Highum, A. C. "Assessing Administrator and Faculty Support for Community College Activities." Paper presented at the Annual Conference of the American Association of Community and Junior Colleges, Washington, D.C., April 1–4, 1984. 17 pp. (ED 242 374).

Details findings of a study conducted at Cuyahoga Community College (Ohio) to assess faculty and administrator opinions concerning the activities that should be undertaken by the college. Describes study methodology, which involved a sixty-six-item survey instrument asking respondents to indicate whether they agreed strongly, agreed, were neutral, disagreed, disagreed strongly, or had no opinion concerning whether particular activities were important and being well done. Notes, among other findings, that faculty were not as likely as administrators to support nontraditional, off-campus classes for local community groups.

Hyde, W. *A New Look at Community College Access.* Denver, Colo.: Education Commission of the States, 1982. 194 pp. (ED 217 905).

Examines key questions related to the provision of educational opportunities by community colleges. Includes individual chapters on the different meanings of educational access, the extent to which community college access has been achieved, the limits to access imposed by financial constraints and conflicting needs, community college practices that affect access, the likely importance of access in the 1980s, and implications. Concludes that the era of access has ended and that it has been replaced with concerns for quality and accountability.

Koltai, L. "Shaping Change: New Goals and New Roles." Paper presented at the Annual Conference of the California Association of Community Colleges Commission on Research, Asilomar, California, April 11–13, 1984. 48 pp. (ED 243 523).

Discusses the crisis of identity facing California's community colleges in light of societal forces influencing or reflecting change. Notes the role of community colleges in expanding access to nontraditional programs, but warns college practitioners that the community college philosophy is not shared by all. Argues that "we have been naive about the social and political consensus which underlies our efforts, and we have been overly self-righteous when our effectiveness was questioned" (p. 5).

Long, J. P. *Vocational-Technical Education in the Community Colleges: A Promising Future.* Columbus: National Center for Research in Vocational Education, Ohio State University, 1984. 14 pp. (ED 246 972).

Examines the current status and future of the community college's role in the delivery of vocational education. Posits a strong place for community colleges in vocational education, but notes that the two-year institutions have played only a limited role in the American Vocational Association (AVA). Argues that history, state governance patterns, and many other factors have all combined to limit the role of postsecondary education in the AVA.

McMullen, H. G. *Community College Business and Industry Educational Partnerships: An Essential Industrial Development Linkage.* Middletown, Va.: Lord Fairfax Community College, 1984. 10 pp. (ED 244 709).

Maintains that Virginia's community colleges could easily be more closely linked to economic and industrial development efforts within the state. Notes that the colleges' educational partnership programs, which have recently been stimulated by government encouragement and intercollegiate cooperation, are ready-made facets of industrial training and provide a reciprocal opportunity for regional economic development on a cooperative basis. Describes the "Educational Partnership Inventory" used by Lord Fairfax Community College to delineate appropriate college and industry contributions in joint endeavors.

Minnesota State Community College Board. *The Strategic Plan of the Minnesota Community College System.* St. Paul: The Board, [1984]. 250 pp. (ED 251 165).

Includes mission and work statements for the Minnesota Community College System (MCCS) and explains plans for dealing with anticipated enrollment fluctuations over the next ten years. Outlines functions of the community colleges and defends their comprehensive mission. Argues that the colleges should not prefer one mission over the other: "Not to try to perform all elements of the missions would be a betrayal of the role community colleges play in serving the citizens of Minnesota" (p. 97). Serves as an example of how one state has defined and defended the comprehensive mission of its community colleges.

National Council of State Directors of Community-Junior Colleges. *Status of Open Door Admissions.* Issues, Trends and Projects Committee Report No. 1. N.P.: The Council, 1983. 35 pp. (ED 230 214).

Describes a survey of state directors of community colleges that was conducted in January 1983 to determine the level of state commitment to the philosophy of open-door access. Examines survey findings as they relate to: (1) the extent to which states have formal written policies expressing commitment to the open door, (2) whether those policies have legal status, (3) the impact of budgetary restraints on open-door admissions, and (4) the role of enrollment projections in the budgetary process. Notes, among other findings, that there is a trend to curtail enrollment through budgeting procedures. Includes a state-by-state analysis of survey responses.

Parsons, M. H. "Technology Transfer: Programs, Procedures, and Personnel." Paper presented at a roundtable at the Annual Convention of the American Association of Community and Junior Colleges, New Orleans, La., April 24–27, 1983. 9 pp. (ED 230 244).

Maintains that all community colleges have the capability of identifying emerging technological innovations and designing delivery systems to transfer these innovations to local businesses and industry. Identifies modes of transferring technology, including: (1) the translations of technical knowledge into information about operational tactics, (2) the installation and application of new hardware, and (3) contracts for the delivery of technological services. Posits a strong community college role in keeping local industries abreast of technological changes.

Richardson, R. C., Jr. "Future of the Open Door: A Presentation for ACCT." Paper presented at the Annual Convention of the Association of Community College Trustees, Phoenix, Arizona, October 12–16, 1983. 8 pp. (ED 235 848).

Argues that the open door of the community college too often becomes a revolving door when student needs are not met and quality decreases. Urges colleges to: (1) define competencies needed for success, (2) assess students at entrance, (3) provide needed remediation, (4) provide accurate information regarding preprograms and changes of admission to programs of original choice, and (5) obtain adequate funding for services provided to underprepared students.

Richardson, R. C., Jr., and Doucette, D. S. "An Empirical Model for Formulating Operational Missions for Community Colleges." Paper presented at the Annual Meeting of the American Educational Research Association, New Orleans, La., April 23–27, 1984. 17 pp. (ED 243 509).

Describes the development and application of the Community College Activities Survey (CCAS), a questionnaire that lists sixty activities undertaken by community colleges and asks respondents to indicate how well each activity is being carried out and how important it is to the college mission. Summarizes major findings of a study in which the CCAS was administered to more than 3,500 persons in Arizona, including governing board members, administrators, faculty, legislators, and registered voters. Notes the usefulness of the study in helping administrators to gauge legislative and public priorities concerning the role of the community college.

Smith, E. M., Roberts, C., Seal, E., Puckett, T., Jagger, B. and Davis, T. *A Study of the Roles and Missions of the Public Junior Colleges of the State of*

Mississippi. Jackson: Mississippi Junior College Association, 1982. 60 pp. (ED 235 863).

Describes a survey of administrators, faculty, trustees, state legislators, and local governmental officials who were asked to rank forty-one goal statements in terms of "what is" and "what should be." Concludes, among other findings, that the economic turndown of the early 1980s has caused many college constitutencies to determine that the goals of low tuition and open access — though still important — should not be one of the top priorities of the junior college in the future. The survey instrument is appended.

Townsend, B. K. "Faculty Role in Classifying the Mission." *Community College Review*, 1984, *12* (2), 4–7.

Notes the unclear or weak identity of the community college within higher education and warns that the lack of a distinct identity will result in lowered tax support and declining enrollments. Argues that in a time of declining financial support, the colleges will have to choose certain missions over others. Urges a strong faculty role in the development of the college identity.

Tyree, L. W., and McConnell, N. C. *Linking Community College with Economic Development in Florida.* ISHE Fellows Program Research Report No. 3, 1982. Tallahassee: Institute for Studies in Higher Education, Florida State University, 1982. 38 pp. (ED 226 785).

Examines the role of community colleges in industrial development, particularly in the area of retraining blue-collar workers from dying, labor-intensive industries. Highlights major factors arguing for strong links between education and industry, including the decline of labor-intensive manufacturing, the rise of high-technology industries, the demographic shift to the sunbelt states, and the need for large-scale retraining programs. Outlines advantages that colleges can offer to industry and provides examples of programs developed in the Carolinas, California and New Jersey.

Vogler, D. E. "Mission Expansion: Business, Industry and Education Involvement." *Community Services Catalyst*, 1984, *14* (4), 4–7.

Argues that it is proper for community colleges to include local economic development efforts within the scope of the college mission. Notes that special programs for business and industry could help fill the gap left by sluggish enrollments. Concludes further that failure to expand into this area would be contrary to the longstanding commitment of colleges to respond to local community needs.

Wattenbarger, J. L. "Maintaining the Vision of the Grail." Paper presented at the Conference of the National Council for Staff, Program and Organizational Development, Overland Park, Kansas, October 30–November 2, 1983. 15 pp. (ED 238 483).

Argues that the traditional, open-door mission of the community college is being challenged indirectly through increased "quality controls" and lowered financial support. Maintains that minimum competency testing may be contrary to the spirit of the community college if testing is used to measure a person's value rather than helping him or her to achieve. Concludes that survival of the open door will require increased attention to the basic college mission and more concern for individual needs.

Williams, B. B., and Atwell, C. A. "Critics of Lifelong Learning: A Reasoned Response." *Community Services Catalyst*, 1984, *14* (2), 5–8.

Outlines criticisms of the community college commitment to low-cost, lifelong education. Argues in response that there is a great societal need for institutions that can respond quickly to the ever changing educational needs of adults. Maintains further that "community colleges are in the best position, from the standpoint of mission, cost, and location, to continue to lead in these efforts" (p. 8).

Assessing the Quality of Community College Education

Quality has become a buzz word in educational circles. Yet relatively few authors examine what is actually meant by quality or how quality can be achieved. The citations listed in this section of the bibliography represent efforts to take on this task.

Bender, L. W. "Differences and Implications of Legislator and Educator Perceptions of Quality Education." Paper presented at the Annual Convention of the California Association of Community Colleges, Sacramento, California, November 18–20, 1983. 15 pp. (ED 237 142).

Reviews differing definitions of educational quality as expressed by educators and legislators. Classifies components of quality into three categories: (1) input, such as student test scores and faculty characteristics; (2) process, such as library resources; and (3) outcomes, such as graduate placement and honors. Reveals that legislators tend to focus on outcomes while educators tend to emphasize the input and process quality indicators, probably due to the educator's desire for job security and the legislator's desire for reelection. Suggests that educators develop an understanding of public opinion and legislative issues, and learn the art of compromise.

Conrad, C. F. "Enhancing Program Quality." *Community College Review*, 1983–84, *11* (3), 15–21.

Provides a review and critique of current institutional approaches to quality in the community and two-year college. Offers suggestions for the enhancement of quality through self-assessment and program design encompassing inputs, outcomes, the educational process, and the integrality of these concepts. Urges a renewed commitment to assessing quality.

de los Santos, A. G., Jr. "Excellent Teaching: The Need for a Corporate Valve, or the Need to Add a Third 'C' in Community College Teaching." Paper presented at the Annual Conference of the National Institute for Staff and Organizational Development on Teaching Excellence, Austin, Texas, May 22–25, 1984. 20 pp. (ED 245 746).

Uses the corporate sector as an example of quality, noting that recent community college literature reveals little about instructional quality. Identifies three characteristics linked to corporate success: (1) concern for customer needs, (2) treating people with respect, and (3) holding to a set of fundamental values. Suggests that application of these characteristics to the community college requires analyzing students' needs, defining quality in terms of needs, showing concern for faculty well-being, and developing programs in line with the institution's values. Argues that teaching excellence is worth the effort of adopting a new corporate value.

Hinkley, B., and others. *Academic Standards: The Faculty's Role. An Academic Senate Position Paper: Discussion and Action*. Sacramento: Academic Senate for California Community Colleges, 1983. 8 pp. (ED 241 079).

Notes a concern among community college faculty over academic standards. Suggests that to re-examine standards, faculty should: (1) discuss the functions of standards in relation to student competency, (2) review departmental course outlines, catalogue descriptions and course implementation, (3) consider selecting textbooks or grading papers together, (4) sponsor cross-disciplinary discussion on standards, (5) involve part-time faculty in discussions, and (6) exhibit faculty professionalism. Concludes that when faculty agree upon standards, they can then uniformly communicate these to students and ensure an appropriately rigorous education.

Losak, J. *Measuring the Impact of Student Assessment on Institutional Quality.* Florida: Miami-Dade Community College, Office of Institutional Research, 1982. 9 pp. (ED 226 782).

Discusses assessment testing at community colleges and its relationship to educational quality. Reveals that two tests, admissions and placement, affect quality by separating high and low achievers, but do not ensure instructional quality. Suggests that exit examinations impact quality more directly by requiring the curriculum to be geared to provide the knowledge to be tested. Identifies two types of exit exams — minimal skills measurement and achievement measures — noting a relationship between expectation and achievement. Argues in favor of achievement tests over minimum skills testing, suggesting that high institutional expectations result in high student performance.

Palmer, J. C. "How Is Quality Measured in the Community College?" *Community College Review*, 1983–84, *11*, 52–62.

Examines literature pertaining to quality at the community college. Identifies five determinants of quality: institutional resources, instructional and management processes, student outcomes, value-added impact on students, and curricular structure and emphasis. Reviews techniques used to measure institutional and program quality including outcome measures, value-added measures, and a decision-making approach. Concludes that educational quality in the community college is closely aligned to the question over the community college's role in higher education.

Vaughan, G. B. "Balancing Open Access and Quality: The Community College at the Watershed." *Change*, 1984, *16* (2), 38–44.

Argues that community colleges face a crisis of identity caused by declining numbers of high school graduates, changes in the community college's national leadership, and the changing economy. Maintains that as colleges evolve in this new era, they should: (1) adhere to the principles of open access and curricular comprehensiveness, (2) maintain institutional integrity in the face of external pressures to change, and (3) prevent faculty and administrator burnout. Notes the barriers administrators will face as they work toward each of these three goals.

Maintaining an Effective Faculty

Community colleges are labor-intensive operations, and nothing is more central to institutional integrity than the performance of the faculty. During the 1960s (when the ERIC system was started) the literature on community college faculty focused on problems associated with filling the large number of teaching positions available and providing new faculty with the teaching skills necessary in the community college setting. Today's literature — as the citations below illustrate — centers on faculty development efforts to revitalize an older, stable faculty and to integrate growing numbers of part-time instructors into the college community.

Armes, N., and Watkins, K. "The Shadow Side of Teaching: An Analysis of Personal Concerns." *Community College Review*, 1983, *11* (2), 13–19.

Discusses common personal concerns of college teachers (time, money, reputation, significance, and the future) as revealed in surveys and conferences. Notes an increased interest in burnout in the profession and relates it to discrepancies between perceptions of what should be and what in fact is. Views escape and disengagement as typical responses.

Caswell, J. M. "Low Cost/High Value Staff Development Program." Paper presented at the Annual Conference of the World Futures Society's Education Section, Dallas, Texas, February 13–16, 1983. 10 pp. (ED 229 088).

Describes the Dallas County Community College District Career Development and Renewal Program that offers career-path training to staff, provides internal promotion opportunities, and broadens employee understanding of community college education. Relates that projects may involve internships, career understudy activities, or special research projects. Notes that there is no current budget for the program and that participants must volunteer their time.

Davis, R. M. "Relevancy and Revitalization: Retaining Quality and Vitality in Two-Year College Mathematics Faculty." Paper presented at the Sloan Foundation Conference on New Directions in Two-Year College Mathematics, Atherton, Calif., July 11–14, 1984. 14 pp. (ED 251 124).

Argues that mathematics faculty need retraining to acquire new knowledge and incorporate new instructional approaches. Warns that faculty vitality, depleted by limited resources and changing student demographics, needs to be uplifted. Urges a new direction on the part of colleges in terms of workload, remuneration and faculty role and calls for broader societal involvement in retaining quality instruction and faculty vitality.

Fox, G. C. "Factors that Motivate Part-Time Faculty." *Community Services Catalyst*, 1984, *14* (1), 17–21.

    Examines a study applying the problem-sensing and idea-generating capacities of the Nominal Group Technique (NGT) in part-time faculty workshops. Outlines the NGT process and its use in identifying the institutional conditions that facilitate and inhibit part-time teachers' effectiveness.

McArthur, K. R. "Occupational Apathy: A Social or Individual Responsibility?" Paper presented at the Annual Spring Meeting of the Community College Social Science Association, San Diego, Calif., March 18, 1983. 10 pp. (ED 229 074).

    Relates instructor apathy to a growing national malaise caused by a lack of clear national goals, increased bureaucracy, the emergence of unions in colleges, and an emphasis on personal rather than organizational priorities. Proposes that instructors have developed the following psychosocial products: learned helplessness, overindulgence, and the inability to modify lifestyles to keep pace with changing needs. Explores ways that teacher apathy resulting from these three products may be overcome by the modification of expectations.

McCright, G. J. "A Study of Perceived Professional Development Needs of Part-Time Faculty Members at Marshalltown Community College." Ed.D. practicum, Nova University, Iowa, 1983. 37 pp. (ED 242 364).

    Reports on a survey of part-time faculty at Marshalltown Community College (Iowa) to determine their professional development needs. Reveals, among other findings, that the respondents indicated the highest level of interest in special recognition for innovative teaching as a professional development incentive. Recommends that part-time instructors be more fully recognized as an important segment of the total instructional staff.

McMullen, H. G., and others. *College Teaching Center: Inventory of Resources and Services. Fourth Edition.* Middletown, Va.: Lord Fairfax Community College, 1982. 39 pp. (ED 225 635).

    Describes the resources and services available to faculty and staff at the College Teaching Center (CTC) of Lord Fairfax Community College. Includes a listing of resources on the study of college teaching, a discussion of projected staff development activities for 1981–83, an annotated bibliography on college teaching, and a list of materials available at

CTC, including assessment tools, resources on instructional development and audio-visual materials.

Maguire, P. "Enhancing the Effectiveness of Adjunct Faculty." *Community College Review*, 1983–84, *11* (3), 27–33.

Argues that if community colleges are to thrive as institutions of higher learning, they must endeavor to integrate adjunct faculty more fully within the institution. Examines some negative outcomes in the use of part-time faculty, including weakened loyalty, lack of morale, and its effect on students. Urges that more energy be channeled into recognizing, understanding, and supporting part-time faculty.

Morton, R. D., and Newman, D. L. "Part-Time Teachers of Community Colleges: Who Are They and Why Do They Teach?" Paper presented at the Annual Meeting of the American Educational Research Association, New Orleans, La., April 23–27, 1984. 15 pp. (ED 244 661)

Reports on a statewide survey of part-time teachers of non-credit community college courses. Reveals that people teach for a variety of reasons and that salary is not always the most important factor. Suggests that administrators use recruitment strategies emphasizing the personal and professional benefits of part-time teaching and communicate to teachers that they are an essential element of the institution.

Parsons, M. H. "Catching Up: Faculty Technological Upgrade through Return to Industry." Paper presented at the Conference of the New Jersey Consortium on the Community College, Inc., on "Vocational Education in the Community College," Atlantic City, N.J., May 19, 1983. 10 pp. (ED 231 451).

Describes Hagerstown Junior College's (Maryland) Return-to-Industry Project that sends occupational faculty to industrial settings to update their skills and knowledge. Reviews procedures for participating in the project and enumerates the benefits of the program, including increased understanding between the college and host industries. Notes that, despite a lack of continuing grant support, the project will be maintained through other funds.

Peterson, T. "Part-Time Faculty Compensation and Staff Development in Three Kansas City Area Community Colleges." Graduate seminar paper, University of Missouri, Kansas City, [1982]. 24 pp. (ED 225 615).

Examines compensation packages and staff development provisions at Johnson County Community College, Kansas City Kansas Community College, and Penn Valley Community College. Confirms conclusions drawn from the literature that part-time faculty are underpaid and neglected in terms of staff development. Includes a literature review, copies of adjunct faculty contracts and a bibliography.

Phillips, H. "The Care and Feeding of Part-Time Teachers." Paper presented at the National Conference of the National Council for Staff, Program and Organizational Development, Atlanta, Ga., October 27–28, 1984. 8 pp. (ED 251 144).

Discusses the role of community college part-time faculty and ways to improve their performance and morale. Outlines the advantages of employing part-time teachers and specifies some of their particular needs: (1) a supportive president, (2) staff development programs, (3) freedom to innovate and experiment, (4) the involvement of part-timers in college activities, and (5) a system of performance evaluation.

Rabalais, M. J., and Penitt, J. E. "Instructional Development for Part-Time Faculty." *Community College Review*, 1983, *11* (2), 20–22.

Describes Hinds Junior College's (Alabama) staff development program for part-time faculty. Points out the features of the program, noting that it includes a general orientation session and four subsequent modules. Reviews evaluations of these sessions, concluding that the program has enhanced faculty awareness of administrative expectations, instructional practices, and of the college itself.

Rohfeld, R. "Faculty Growth Through Community Development." *Community Services Catalyst*, 1984, *14* (1), 8–11.

Discusses faculty involvement in the community as a means of faculty development. Enumerates ways institutions can benefit from faculty involvement in community development. Sees community involvement as one way to meet faculty members' need for job enrichment. Identifies possible community development activities, requisite skills, and ways instructors can develop these skills.

Shawl, W. F. "Staff Development: A New Imperative." Paper presented at the Annual Convention of the American Association of Community and Junior Colleges, Washington, D.C., April 1–4, 1984. 17 pp. (ED 243 512).

Discusses effects of retrenchment on community college faculty and calls for faculty development programs. Notes that when junior faculty members are often laid off, the remaining, more experienced instructors may not fit the needs of a smaller curriculum. Suggests that community colleges devote a substantial amount of their resources to research and development in order to deliver higher instructional quality at lower costs. Advocates incentives for faculty to develop new skills, keep up in their fields, and, if necessary, retrain.

Shawl, W. F. "Professional Development Programs That Work." Paper presented at the Annual Convention of the American Association of Community and Junior Colleges, Washington, D.C., April 1–4, 1984. 17 pp. (ED 243 513).

Identifies factors leading to the success of the professional development program at Golden West College (California) and discusses elements in planning staff development programs. Suggests that planners of staff development programs: (1) locate a convenient office, (2) minimize administrative detail, (3) reward participants, (4) gain administrative support, (5) establish programs responding to large and small needs, (6) join a staff development network, and (7) involve the whole campus in the effort.

Venitsky, J. L. "Using Videotape for Self-Improvement. Instructional Innovation Monograph." Paper prepared for the Annual California Great Teachers Seminar, Santa Barbara, Calif., August 20–25, 1982. 9 pp. (ED 224 549).

Discusses the use of video recorders to strengthen communication skills for both faculty and students through self-evaluation and self-improvement. Identifies three principles of effective media use: the extensive use of positive reinforcement; the provision of immediate and private feedback; and the provision for multiple recorded experiences, each building upon the proceeding one. Points out that faculty and students, given the power to see and hear themselves as others do, can be motivated to achieve more effective communication skills.

Winter, G., and others. *Faculty Development Manual for Adjunct Staff in Postsecondary Occupational Programs.* Albany: State University of New York, Two Year College Development Center, 1981. 75 pp. (ED 233 777).

Presents a collection of ideas and resources on faculty development programs for adjunct staff in postsecondary occupational education. Provides a perspective on disadvantages facing adjunct faculty and a model to assist in program development. Outlines seven inservice programs/activities, detailing objectives, materials, and schedules. Suggests that nonprogram, inservice activities utilize the buddy system, department integration, adjunct faculty organizations, and newsletters.

The Effects and Management of Retrenchment

The number of documents on retrenchment has tapered off since the late 1970s; discussions of appropriate responses to budget cuts have given way to a growing number of authors who examine long-range strategic planning. Nonetheless, the threat of fiscal cutbacks and the threats those cutbacks pose to institutional integrity are a major theme in the literature.

This section reviews those authors who examine the consequences of fiscal cutbacks and strategies taken by administrators to manage retrenchment. These documents demonstrate that retrenchment results in more than smaller staffs and limited services. It shrinks the mission of the community college back to the traditional credit curriculum and severely limits the community services and outreach functions.

Arth, M. P. "Planning and Budgeting in a Period of Resource Constraint: The New Climate." *Planning For Higher Education*, 1984, *12* (3), 1–8.

Argues that "the very nature of the planning and budgeting process is affected by the resource environment in which planning and budgeting take place" (p. 1). Demonstrates this thesis by reference to practices at Cuyahoga Community College (Ohio). Concludes that budgeting becomes more of a political process—and less of a professional and technical process—when budgets are reduced.

Broussal, L. R. "Community College Noncredit Programming: The Tractable Educational Resource." Unpublished paper, [1984]. 11 pp. (ED 253 265).

Focuses on noncredit programming in the San Francisco Community College District (California) and the threats to those activities posed by recent funding reductions. Examines and argues against the trend favoring traditional programming over nontraditional education in the perennial battle for funding. Notes that California's Proposition 13 had a particularly deleterious effect on noncredit adult and continuing education.

California Postsecondary Education Commission. *Impact of 1982-83*

Budget Constraints on the California Community Colleges: Results of a Commission Survey. Commission Report 83–28. Sacramento: The Commission, 1983. 27 pp. (ED 234 857).

Details findings of a survey conducted in Spring 1983 to inventory the actions taken by the California community colleges in response to 1982–83 budget limitations. Notes, among other findings, that: (1) 95 percent of the colleges reduced course offerings; (2) 41 percent reduced student outreach, recruitment, and public information efforts; and (3) 52 percent reduced the number of off-campus locations. Concludes that budget constraints have threatened the scope and quality of California's community colleges.

Casey, J. W. *Managing Contraction: An Institution Experiences Contraction. Seattle Community College District, Seattle, Washington, U.S.A.* Seattle: Seattle Community College District, 1982. 17 pp. (ED 229 064).

Describes a four-stage sequence for retrenchment which involves: (1) reduction of services on a somewhat proportional basis, (2) disproportionate cutback of particular services, (3) cutbacks in whole categories of programs and services, and (4) the reformulation of the college's mission to cope with retrenchment. Concludes that community colleges are particularly vulnerable in bad economic times because they are relativewly new to higher education.

Hayward, G. C. *Consequences of 1983–84 Budget Cuts for California Community Colleges.* Sacramento: Office of the Chancellor, California Community Colleges, 1983. 24 pp. (ED 232 746).

Examines the consequences of a gubernatorial veto of the 1983–84 Budget Bill which amounted to a cut of $232 million, eliminating the funding necessary to implement equalization, inflation, and growth provisions in community college funding. Notes that the results of the budget cut will include the cancellation of 15,000 course sections statewide, the inability of colleges to improve student retrenchment through better assessment and counseling, and other reductions in services and personnel.

Hicks, W. B. "Survey on the Effects of State Budget Cuts on Community College Learning Resource Centers: A Narrative Survey." Paper presented at the Annual Northern and Southern California Meetings of the Learning Resources Association of California Community Colleges, 1984. 13 pp. (ED 244 662).

Examines the findings of a survey conducted to profile learning resources centers in California in terms of personnel, budget, service cuts, budget ideas, long-range plans, and funding mechanisms. Notes that 86 percent of the respondents reported reductions in personnel, representing a total loss of 209 full-time positions. Also points out that the largest reductions in budget items were for library equipment, audiovisual materials and television equipment.

Keyser, J. S. "Budgetary Decline: Asking the Right Questions." *Community College Review*, 1984, *12* (1), 32–35.

Describes efforts undertaken at Linn-Benton Community College (Oregon) to develop priority-based contingency plans for a reduced budget using information provided by division directors on their program's relationship to college mission, instructional costs, graduates' employment outlook, follow-up data, enrollments, sunk costs, and other areas. Lists thirteen questions the division heads are required to answer in providing information about their programs.

Lawrence, B. "Beyond the Bottom Line: Good Managers Look to Results." *Community and Junior College Journal*, 1984, *54* (5), 21–23.

Reviews findings of a National Center for Higher Education Management Systems (NCHEMS) study, which investigated the effects of enrollment and revenue declines on small independent four-year colleges. Discusses implications for two-year colleges facing similar problems and looks at strategies that helped more resilient colleges meet financial problems.

Murphy, M. T. *Policies and Procedures Relating to Program Redirection and Financial Exigency.* Bel Air, Md.: Harford Community College, 1983. 16 pp. (ED 227 910).

Outlines policies that have been developed at Harford Community College (Maryland) to (1) monitor current and projected expenditures relative to accrued benefits and (2) reduce or redirect expenditures and personnel in the event of declines in enrollment or revenues. Identifies three levels of adjustment that may be implemented by the president to ensure the judicious use of resources: adjustments to ongoing operations, program change or reduction, and a declaration of financial exigency which may require severance of regular employees.

Nichols, D. D., and Stuart, W. H. "In Praise of Fewer Administrators." Paper prepared for the American Association of Community and Junior Colleges, Washington, D. C., [1983]. 26 pp. (ED 227 889).

Describes the efforts of Oakland Community College (Michigan) to reduce staff costs by decreasing the number of college administrators. Notes that this policy was accomplished through the consolidation of job functions, a commitment not to fill jobs which were vacated, and a policy of eliminating services to the college and community that could not be justified financially.

Petersen, A. L. *Courses to be Deleted from the Credit and Noncredit Program of the Community Colleges.* Sacramento: Board of Governors, California Community Colleges, 1982. 11 pp. (ED 217 959).

Describes the procedures employed in deleting courses from the credit and noncredit programs of the California community colleges in response to a $30 million deduction from total community college apportionments. Notes that criteria for deletion focus on courses which do not assist in the fulfillment of college missions, those in which students enroll for mainly private interest, those which should be offered on a fee basis, and those whose deletion would not inhibit a college's responsiveness to business or industry needs.

The State Role in Community College Education

State government, through legislation and coordinating commissions, plays a central role in the institutional integrity of community colleges. The ERIC documents listed in this section of the bibliography illustrate the variety of ways in which this state role is exercised: regulations governing personnel policies; long-range statewide planning; program evaluation and institutional recognition; statewide funding mechanisms; and standards of academic progress for students. It should be noted, however, that while many authors describe the mechanisms of state control, relatively few study its actual effects.

Academic Senate for California Community Colleges. *Hiring and Evaluation.* Sacramento: Academic Senate for California Community Colleges, [1983.] 40 pp. (ED 238 495).

Reviews state legal provisions and regulations relating to the hiring and evaluation of certified community college staff in California. Presents sections of Article 2 of the California Education Code and outlines recommendations focusing on such areas as the clear definition of hiring procedures, faculty participation in selection, regular and timely evaluation of administrators, and the development by faculty of a definition of competence. Presents information that is designed to assist local academic senates in developing or updating personnel policies.

California Community Colleges. *Evaluating Statewide Priorities. Improving Community College Evaluation and Planning:* Project Working Paper no. 9. Sacramento: Office of the Chancellor, California Community Colleges; Aptos, Calif.: Western Association of Schools and Colleges, Accrediting Commission for Community and Junior Colleges, 1983. 36 pp. (ED 250 043).

Provides a working paper intended for use by twenty community colleges in California undergoing accreditation self-studies during 1982–83. Notes that the colleges were asked to evaluate their performance with respect to statewide priorities and standards relating to: (1) open admission, (2) opportunities for individual enrollment determined by student readiness and willingness to learn, (3) instructional excellence, (4) articulated transfer programs, (5) vocational education, (6) student guidance and support services, (7) remedial education, and (8) community services and continuing education.

Florida State Department of Education. *CLAST: College Level Academic Skills Test. Test Administration Plan, 1983–84.* Tallahassee: Florida State Department of Education, 1984. 35 pp. (ED 242 344).

Provides information on the terms and conditions governing the administration of the College Level Academic Skills Test (CLAST), an instrument designed to measure the achievement of the communication and computation skills expected of all students by the time they complete their sophomore year. Includes information on eligibility to take CLAST, registration of examinees, requests to take CLAST in another institution, scoring conventions, reporting test results, reporting and use of CLAST scores, student appeals, retake policies, and investigation of alleged irregularities. Also includes a description of the test.

Illinois Community College Board. *Recognition Manual for Illinois Public Community Colleges.* Springfield: Illinois Community College Board, 1983. 36 pp. (ED 250 052).

Describes the process by which a college becomes recognized by the Illinois Community College Board. Also examines the criteria upon which recognition decisions are made, describes the effects of such decisions, and explains how they may be appealed. Appendices include recognition standards, a copy of the application for recognition, and a schedule of recognition visits for 1983 through 1985.

Malcolm-Rodgers, R. *Maryland Community Colleges Continuing Education Manual.* Annapolis: Maryland State Board for Community Colleges, 1983. 85 pp. (ED 234 851).

Presents policies for state participation in continuing education courses and highlights evaluation criteria for those courses, including those submitted for state funding and those for which state funding is not required. Includes instructions for the completion of various forms required for state funding and details the annual community college continuing education reporting schedule.

Martorana, S. V., and Garland, P. H. *Highlights and Overview of Actions in 1983 State Legislative Sessions Affecting Community and Two-Year Technical Colleges: A Report to the National Council of State Directors of Community and Junior Colleges.* University Park: Center for the Study of Higher Education, Pennsylvania State University, 1984. 19 pp. (ED 246 945).

Reviews the quantity and types of state legislation concerning two-year colleges in 1983. Reveals, among other findings, that: (1) 1,127 pieces of legislation were introduced and that of these, 54 percent had been enacted; (2) financial and administrative issues were the major legislative concerns; and (3) the amount of legislation increased by 29 percent over 1982. Serves as a useful overview of the extent of state legislative influence over community colleges.

Maryland State Board for Community Colleges. *State Plan and Annual Report: Tenth Annual Community College Plan.* Annapolis: Maryland State Board for Community Colleges, 1983. 199 pp. (ED 233 766).

Serves as a source of current information on and as a guide to future activities in Maryland's community colleges. Notes trends, goals, and needs of the colleges; discusses the system's statewide governance structure; and considers state and local coordination. Also reviews the goals and objectives of the Maryland State Board for Community Colleges and examines implementation strategies.

Maryland State Board for Community Colleges. *Study of State Funding of Maryland Community Colleges, 1984.* Annapolis: Maryland State Board for Community Colleges, 1984. 62 pp. (ED248 943).

Describes a study undertaken to examine the funding of Maryland's community college system and to develop an improved funding approach that would take into account differences in local wealth. Includes appendices that provide financial data, information on funding mechanisms used in other states, and proposed legislation.

Michigan State Department of Education. *MiSIS (Michigan Student Information System) Activities Manual.* Lansing: Higher Education Management Services, Michigan State Department of Education, 1979. 92 pp. (ED 234 831).

Details each of the six subsystems of the Michigan Student Information System (MiSIS), the student flow component of Michigan's statewide system for evaluating occupational education. Discusses the objectives, assumptions, and development of MiSIS as well as the national and state laws that have reporting requirements for which MiSIS data may be used. Includes copies of the actual instruments used in the MiSIS data collection process.

Nespoli, L. A. *Maryland Community Colleges 1983 Program Evaluations.* Annapolis: Maryland State Board for Community Colleges, 1984. 186 pp. (ED 243 531).

Contains the results of individual qualitative evaluations of fortyeight community college programs throughout the state as well as the results of a statewide evaluation of criminal justice and law enforcement programs. Serves as an example of the state role in program evaluation. Notes that in the evaluation process colleges are required to respond to questions related to problems such as high or increasing program costs, dwindling enrollment, or low student transfer rates.

Nussbaum, T. *Minimum Standards for Instructional Programs, Faculty and Facilities.* Sacramento: Office of the Chancellor, California Community Colleges, 1983. 25 pp. (ED 234 864).

Highlights recommendations to the Board of Governors of the California Community Colleges for new minimum standards in the areas of instructional programs, faculty and facilities. Recommendations for instructional programs cover program objectives, course and program approval, curriculum balance, program review, articulation with high schools and four-year institutions, information dissemination, academic calendar, criteria for credit and noncredit courses, class size, and program priorities.

Simpson, J. R., and Clowes, D. A. (Eds.). *Virginia Community Colleges in the Eighties. [Proceedings of a Conference.] (Blacksburg, Virginia, September 22–23, 1980).* Dublin, Va.: New River Community College; Blacksburg, Va.: Community College Program Area, Virginia Polytechnic Institute and State University, 1981. 102 pp. (ED 231 411).

Reviews issues likely to affect the community colleges in Virginia in the 1980s. Includes discussions of the role of the State Council of Higher Education and its perspectives on the coming decade, legislative and public policies affecting different sectors of education in the state, trends in the Virginia Community College System, and external concerns and challenges faced by the colleges.

Smith, M. L. *A Study of the Status of Tenure in the Nation's Public Two-Year Colleges.* San Marcos: Southwest Texas State University, 1984. 9 pp. (ED 250 029).

Reports findings of a study conducted to assess the current status of tenure at public two-year colleges. Draws on a survey of state administrators of two-year college education who were asked to provide information on the provision of statutory or customary tenure, the number of years of consecutive employment needed to become eligible for tenure, reasons for dismissal of tenured faculty, and the power of local boards to establish tenure policy. Notes, among other findings, that seven states provided statutory tenure and that in another four states, state governing boards developed statewide tenure policies.

Virginia State Board for Community Colleges. *Virginia Community College System Master Plan, 1982–1990.* Richmond: Virginia State Board for Community Colleges and the Virginia State Department of Community Colleges, 1983. 449 pp. (ED 241 087).

Provides a master plan for Virginia's twenty-three comprehensive community colleges. Examines the master planning process itself and then discusses (among other topics) the organization of the community college system in Virginia and actions of the state board on the system's mission, goals, planning assumptions, and strategic objectives. Includes a summary of existing and proposed programs and standardized criteria for program planning.

Washington State Board for Community College Education. *Washington State Community College Program and Enrollment Plan, 1985–90. Management Summary.* Olympia: Washington State Board for Community College Education, [1984.] 93 pp. (ED 251 146).

Provides information about the types and magnitude of educational services to be provided by Washington State's community colleges from 1985 to 1990. Includes discussions of the purpose of the plan, the planning process, and improvements needed in the areas of instructional equipment, basic skills instruction, faculty and staff development, and other elements of college operation. Also includes a general statement of priorities.

Jim Palmer is assistant director for user services at the ERIC Clearinghouse for Junior Colleges and a staff associate at the Center for the Study of Community Colleges.

Diane Zwemer is user services librarian at the ERIC Clearinghouse for Junior Colleges.

Index

A

Access. *See* Open access
Administrators, and burnout, 57–58, 59–60
Admissions, and open access, 27
Alabama, faculty vitality in, 91
Alaska State Commission on Postsecondary Education, 64, 74
Alfred, R. L., 78–79
Altschuler, T. C., 49–61
American Association of Community and Junior Colleges, 10, 13, 14, 37, 78, 79
American Association of Junior Colleges, 4, 9, 13
American Association of State Colleges and Universities, 27
American Council on Education, 40
American Vocational Association, 81
Angel, D., 71–72, 74
Arizona, mission in, 79, 83
Armenta, R. R., 78, 79
Armes, N., 88
Aronson, E., 50, 61
Arth, M. P., 93
Atwell, C. A., 78, 85
Austen, J., 51

B

Bender, L. W., 65–66, 70, 74, 85–86
Bess, J., 41
Blake, P. D., 74
Boss, R. S., 78, 79
Brick, M., 4, 9, 14
Broomal, J. K., 65, 68, 74
Broussal, L. R., 93
Brown v. *Board of Education*, and access, 19
Burnout: and administrators, 57–58, 59–60; analysis of, 49–61; causes of, 50–53; concept of, 50; institutional responsibilities for, 56–57; responses to, 55–56; signs of, 53–54; and teaching emphasis, 60
Business, intrusions from, 29–30

C

California: coordination in, 33, 96–97, 99; faculty vitality in, 92; mission in, 79–80, 81, 84; quality in, 86; retrenchment in, 93–95, 96; transfer students in, 10, 79–80
California at Berkeley, University of, historical role of, 8
California Community Colleges, 96–97, 99
California Postsecondary Education Commission, 93–94
Campbell, R., 65, 74
Carnegie Corporation, 13
Casey, J. W., 94
Caswell, J. M., 88
Central Arizona College, and mission, 79
Chicago, University of, historical role of, 6, 7
City University of New York: and open access, 20; parttime faculty at, 43–44
Clark, B. R., 23, 28
Claxton, P. P., 9
Clowes, D. A., 99–100
Cohen, A. M., 78, 79–80
College Level Academic Skills Test, 97
Colorado, coordination in, 32
Community College Activities Survey, 83
Community College Goals Inventory, 80
Community colleges: architects of, 6–9; burnout responsibilities of, 56–57; development of, 9–11; early forms of, 5–6; forces leading to, 4; forerunners of, 4; foundations of, 3–5; functions of, historically, 6–7, 8, 11, 12–13; history of, 3–15; modern growth of, 11–13; and open access, 20; orientation to, for parttime faculty, 44–45; reassessment of, 13–14
Comprehensiveness, and open access, 20–21, 25
Connecticut, coordination in, 32, 66
Conrad, C. F., 86

103

Cooling out function, 23, 79
Corbett, P. C., 65, 68, 74
Cosand, J., 78, 80
Creamer, D. G., 54, 60
Cross, K. P., 13–14
Cuyahoga Community College: and mission, 80–81; and retrenchment, 93

D

Dallas County Community College District, Career Development and Renewal Program of, 88
Darnowski, V. S., 65, 66, 68–69, 74
Davies, G. K., 29–36
Davis, R. M., 88
Davis, T., 83–84
de los Santos, A. G., Jr., 86
Developmental education, and open access, 26
Dewey, J., 8
Doucette, D. S., 78, 83
Dundalk Community College, and mission, 80

E

Educational Partnership Inventory, 82
Educational Testing Service, 43
Eells, W. C., 4, 10–11, 13, 14
Elgin Community College, parttime faculty at, 43
Eliason, N. C., 38
Ernst, R. J., 40–41, 47

F

Faculty: analysis of vitality of, 49–61; and curricular changes, 52–53, 54–55, 58; elitist, 51–52; parttime, 37–47; professional community for, 55, 59; recognition for, 55, 59; reluctant, 50; repetition and boredom for, 52; sources and information on, 87–93; survival tactics of, 53–55; variety for, 58–59
Family background, and open access, 27–28
Financial aid, and open access, 26–27
Financing, alternative techniques for, 33–35
Florida: coordination in, 97; faculty vitality in, 57, 58–59; mission in, 84

Florida State Department of Education, 97
Folwell, W. W., 5, 6
Fox, G. C., 89
Franklin, B., 4
Friedlander, J., 43, 47

G

Gappa, J. M., 37, 40, 41, 42, 43, 45, 47
Garland, P. H., 65, 67, 68, 74, 98
German universities, impact of, 5, 8
GI Bill of Rights, 12, 18–19
Golden West College, faculty at, 92
Goodwin, G. L., 10, 11, 12, 14
Goshen, Indiana, historical institution in, 6
Gunne, G. M., 37, 38, 42, 44, 47

H

Hagerstown Junior College, Return-to-Industry Project of, 90
Harford Community College, and retrenchment, 95
Harnish, D., 54, 60
Harper, W. R., 5, 6–7, 8, 14
Harris, D. A., 40
Harrison, W. L., 78, 80
Hayward, G. C., 94
Heller, D., 49, 60
Hicks, W. B., 94–95
Higher Education Acts, 13, 20
Highum, A. C., 78, 80–81
Hinds Junior College, faculty at, 91
Hinkley, B., 86
Hodgson, G., 12, 14
Hyde, W., 78, 81

I

Idaho, coordination in, 32
Illinois: coordination in, 97; historical institutions in, 4, 6–7; parttime faculty in, 43
Illinois Community College Board, 97
Indiana, historical institution in, 6
Instruction, quality of, and parttime faculty, 41–44
Integrity: and business intrusions, 29–30; concept of, 72; and faculty vitality, 49–61; and mission, search for, 3–15; and open access, 17–28; and parttime faculty, 37–47; sources and informa-

tion for, 77–101; and state intrusions, 30–33; state protection of, 33–36; and state systems, 63–75; threats to, 29–36

Iowa, faculty vitality in, 89

J

Jagger, B., 83–84
Jefferson, T., 4
Johnson County Community College, and faculty, 90–91
Joliet Junior College, historical role of, 4, 6
Jordan, D. S., 5, 7–8, 14

K

Kafka, F., 32
Kansas City Kansas Community College, and faculty, 90–91
Karabel, J., 22–23, 28
Karfy, D., 50, 61
Kellams, S. E., 37, 38, 41, 42, 44, 47
Kellogg Foundation, 13, 79
Kentucky, coordination in, 32
Keyser, J. S., 95
Kintzer, F. C., 65, 66–67, 74
Koltai, L., 78, 81
Koos, L. V., 10, 11, 14
Kyre, K. K., 41, 47

L

LaGuardia Community College, part-time faculty at, 43–44
Lange, A. F., 5, 7, 8, 15
Lasell Female Seminary (Lasell Junior College), historical role of, 4
Lawrence, B., 95
Leslie, D., 37, 38, 40, 41, 42, 44, 47
Lester, P., 75
Lewis Institute, historical role of, 4
Linn-Benton Community College, and retrenchment, 95
Long, J. P., 78, 81
Lord Fairfax Community College: College Teaching Center at, 89–90; and mission, 82
Losak, J., 87

M

McArthur, K. R., 89
McCabe, R. H., 3, 15, 57
McConnell, N. C., 78, 84
McCright, G. J., 89
McDowell, F. M., 9, 15
McFarlane, L. A., 40–41, 47
McGaughey, J. L., 37–47
McMullen, H. G., 78, 82, 89–90
Maguire, P., 90
Malcolm-Rodgers, R., 97–98
Maricopa Community Colleges, and mission, 79
Marshalltown Community College, faculty at, 89
Martorana, S. V., 65, 67, 68, 74, 98
Maryland: coordination in, 32, 97–98, 99; faculty vitality in, 90; historical institution in, 4; mission in, 80; retrenchment in, 95
Maryland State Board for Community Colleges, 98
Massachusetts: coordination in, 32; historical institutions in, 4
Medsker, L. L., 12–13, 15
Miami-Dade Community College, faculty vitality at, 57, 58–59
Michigan: coordination in, 33, 98–99; historical role of, 5; retrenchment in, 95–96
Michigan, University of, and early junior colleges, 5
Michigan State Department of Education, 98–99
Michigan Student Information System, 98–99
Miner, N., 66, 75
Minnesota, University of, and early junior colleges, 5
Minnesota Community College System, and mission, 82
Minnesota State Community College Board, 78, 82
Mission: importance of, 72–73; and open access, 28; sources and information on, 78–85
Mississippi, mission in, 84
Morrill, J., 4
Morrill Act of 1862, 18
Morton, R. D., 90
Mundt, J. C., 66, 75
Murphy, M. T., 95

N

National Center for Education Statistics, 37, 38
National Center for Higher Education Management Systems, 95
National Council of State Directors of Community-Junior Colleges, 78, 82
National Defense Education Act of 1958, 13
Nespoli, L. A., 99
New Jersey: coordination in, 32; mission in, 84
New York: open access in, 20; parttime faculty in, 43–44
Newman, D. L., 90
Newton, Maryland, historical institution in, 4
Nichols, D. D., 95–96
Nominal Group Technique, 89
North Carolina: coordination in, 33; mission in, 84
North Virginia Community College, parttime faculty at, 40–41
Nussbaum, T., 99

O

Oakland Community College, and retrenchment, 95–96
Ohio: mission in, 80–81; retrenchment in, 93
Open access: and admissions, 27; analysis of, 17–28; background on, 17–18; and community colleges, 20; and comprehensiveness, 20–21, 25; criticisms of, 22–23; destroying, 23–24; and developmental education, 26; evolution of, 18–20; and family background, 27–28; and financial aid, 26–27; maintaining, 25–28; and mission, 28; misunderstandings of, 21–22; need for, 24–25; and quality, 27; and tuition, 26
Open door, metaphor of, 21–22
Oregon, retrenchment in, 95

P

Palinchak, R., 4, 15
Palmer, J., 77–101
Parsons, M. H., 38, 40, 47, 78, 82–83, 90

Parttime faculty: analysis of, 37–47; background on, 37–38; institutional integration of, 44–45; and instructional quality, 41–44; motivations of, 42–43; number of, 37–38; rationales for, 38–39; recruitment and selection of, 40–41; roles and functions of, 46–47; summary on, 45–47
Penitt, J. E., 91
Penn Valley Community College, and faculty, 90–91
Pennsylvania State University, Center for the Study of Higher Education at, 67
Petersen, A. L., 96
Peterson, T., 90–91
Philadelphia Academy, historical role of, 4
Phillips, H., 91
Pines, A. M., 50, 61
President's Commission on Higher Education for American Democracy, 12, 15, 19
Puckett, T., 83–84
Putting America Back to Work Project, 79
Puyear, D. E., 1, 63–75

Q

Quality: and open access, 27; and parttime faculty, 41–44; sources and information on, 85–87

R

Rabalais, M. J., 91
Rajasekhara, K., 78, 80
Retrenchment, sources and information on, 93–96
Richardson, R. C., Jr., 78, 79, 83
Richter, S. L., 49–61
Roberts, C., 83–84
Rockefeller Foundation, 6
Rohfeld, R., 91
Roueche, J., 57, 61

S

San Francisco Community College District, and retrenchment, 93
Seal, E., 83–84
Seattle Community College District, and retrenchment, 94

Servicemen's Readjustment Act of 1944, 12, 18–19
Shawl, W. F., 91–92
Shula, D., 49
Simpson, J. R., 99–100
Smith, E. M., 78, 83–84
Smith, M. L., 100
Smutz, W. D., 65, 67, 74
South Carolina, mission in, 84
Stalcup, R., 65, 66, 75
Stanford University, historical role of, 7
State Council of Higher Education for Virginia, coordination by, 31, 99
States: and alternative financing techniques, 33–35; analysis of systems of, 63–75; central agencies of, 68–69; control by, increasing, 65–67; coordinating boards of, 69–72; intrusions by, 30–33; and legislative intervention, 67–68; nature of control by, 67–72; organizational variety among, 64; protections by, 33–36; sources and information on, 96–101; and telecommunication networks, 35–36
Storr, R. J., 7, 15
Stuart, W. H., 95–96
Student Instructional Report, 43–44

T

Tappen, H. P., 5, 6
Telecommunication, state networks for, 35–36
Texas, faculty vitality in, 57, 88
Texas, University of, excellence study at, 57
Townsend, B. K., 78, 84
Truman Commission, 12, 19
Tuckman, H. P., 40, 47
Tuition, and open access, 26
Tyree, L. W., 78, 84

U

U.S. Bureau of Education, 9

V

Vaughan, G. B., 1, 3, 12, 15, 17–28, 72, 73, 75, 87
Venitsky, J. L., 92
Virginia: comprehensive educational system in, 4; coordination in, 31, 32, 68, 69, 99–100; faculty vitality in, 89–90; mission in, 82; parttime faculty in, 40–41; tuition and enrollment in, 26
Virginia Community College System, and coordination, 100
Virginia State Board for Community Colleges, 100; employment criteria of, 41; legislative impact on, 68
Vogler, D. E., 78, 84
Volkwein, J. F., 33, 36

W

Wagoner, J. L., Jr., 3–15, 72
Washington: coordination in, 32, 100–101; retrenchment in, 94
Washington State Board for Community College Education, 100–101
Watkins, K., 88
Wattenbarger, J. L., 78, 85
Wiebe, R. H., 6, 15
Williams, B. B., 78, 85
Wilson, J., 75
Winter, G., 92–93
Wisconsin, coordination in, 32, 33
Wood, J. M., 9

Z

Zoglin, M. L., 65, 75
Zwemer, D., 77–101